Read & Relate

S Forsyth T Bacciarelli A Forsyth
J Ward

Oliver & Boyd

Acknowledgements
The author and publishers acknowledge with thanks permission to reproduce copyright material as follows:

African Universities Press for 'Telephone Conversation' by Wole Soyinka from *Reflections: Nigerian Prose and Verse* ed. Frances Ademola, Pilgrim Books Ltd.; Allen & Unwin for 'The Olympic Ideal' by Richard Stilgoe from *The Richard Stilgoe Letters*; Associated Book Publishers (UK) Ltd. for *Class* by Jilly Cooper, Methuen; The Bodley Head Ltd. for 'The Man in Asbestos: an Allegory of the Future' by Stephen Leacock from *Nonsense Novels*. Reprinted by permission. Campbell Thomson & McLaughlin Ltd. for the extract from *Perfection City* by David Shellan © 1969, by permission of the author. Jonathan Cape Ltd. for *Roots* by Arnold Wesker from *The Wesker Trilogy*; Chatto & Windus Ltd. and The Hogarth Press for 'Assisi' by Norman McCaig from *Surroundings*; Andre Deutsch for 'Pigtail' by Tadeusz Rosewicz from *Faces of Anxiety*; Faber & Faber for 'My Parents Kept Me' by Stephen Spender from *Collected Poems*; 'Scotland's Winter' and 'The Horses' by Edwin Muir from *The Collected Poems of Edwin Muir*; 'The Death of the Ball Turret Gunner' by Randall Jarrell from *The Complete Poems*; 'The Unknown Citizen' by W. H. Auden from *Collected Poems*. John Farquharson Ltd. for 'Eugenesis' by William McIlvanney; Farrar, Strauss & Giroux Inc. for 'After You My Dear Alphonse' by Shirley Jackson; The Estate of Lewis Grassic Gibbon for *Sunset Song* by Lewis Grassic Gibbon; Michael Hamburger for 'Hiroshima' by Jorg Steiner; Hamish Hamilton for *When the Wind Blows* by Raymond Briggs. William Heinemann Ltd. for *Of Mice and Men* by John Steinbeck; David Higham Associates Ltd. for *Room at the Top* by John Braine; Reny McBurney for 'Child with Malaria' by Clark Mills; Memory Lane Music Ltd. for 'My Blue Heaven' by George Whiting; The Estate of the late Sonia Brownell Orwell and Secker & Warburg Ltd. for 'Marrakech', *The Sporting Spirit* and *The Road to Wigan Pier* by George Orwell; Oxford University Press for 'Vergissmeinnicht' by Keith Douglas © Marie J. Douglas, 1978; Penguin Books Ltd. for *Genocide* by Leo Kuper (Pelican Books, 1981) © Leo Kuper, 1981. Laurence Pollinger Ltd. and the Estate of Mrs Frieda Lawrence Ravogli for 'How Beastly the Bourgeois Is' by D. H. Lawrence; George Sassoon for 'They' by Siegfried Sassoon. Reprinted by permission. Tessa Sayle for 'The Other John Peel' from *The Ragman's Daughter* by Alan Sillitoe © 1959, 1960, 1961, 1962, 1963, 1976, Alan Sillitoe; Syndication International Ltd. for *Dateline Cambodia* by John Pilger; The Trustees of the National Library of Scotland for 'A Parable' by William Soutar; Judah Waten for extract from 'The Knife'; Wayland for 'I Have a Dream' by Dr. Martin Luther King; The New Yorker Magazine Inc. for 'The Test' by Angelica Gibbs. Reprinted by permission; © 1940, 1968.

The authors and publishers are grateful to the following for illustrations and use of photographs:

Tony Munro, Andrew Brown, Tony Morris, David Mostyn, John Marshall, Jacqueline Stevenson, Bob Geary and Barry Wilkinson.

Andes Press Agency p. 51; BBC Hulton Picture Library pp. 5, 7, 16, 41, 46, 92, 95, 142; Camera Press pp. 24, 34, 98, 100, 102; Christian Aid p. 48; Douglas Corrance pp. 24, 51; Glasgow Museums and Art Galleries p. 10; Imperial War Museum p. 84; National Trust for Scotland p. 90; Paul Popper Ltd. pp. 22, 37, 69, 80, 92, 105.

Oliver & Boyd
Robert Stevenson House
1–3 Baxter's Place
Leith Walk
Edinburgh EH1 3BB

A division of Longman Group UK Ltd.

ISBN 0 05 004047 2
First published 1989.

Set in Linotron Optima 10 on 12pt and Univers Light 10 on 12pt.
Produced by Longman Group (FE) Ltd
Printed in Hong Kong

Contents

Unit 1

Dreams of a Better World

IDEALISM

What the dictionary says:

ideal: existing in idea; existing in imagination only; highest and best conceivable; perfect as opposed to the real, the imperfect; the highest conception of anything; a standard of perfection.

idealism: a tendency towards the highest conceivable perfection, love for or search after the best and highest.

idealist: one who strives after the ideal; an impractical person.

Utopia: an imaginary state described in Sir Thomas More's *Utopia* (1516). Any imaginary state of ideal perfection.

If you read carefully what the dictionary says, you will see that it describes two ideas:

1 that the *ideal* world is the *perfect* one, and the *real* world is *imperfect*;
2 that the idealist is not only a *dreamer*, but perhaps an impractical person i.e. a person who tries to do something that can't be done or that isn't worth doing.

Before you start to discuss whether you agree with these implications, think about these two short quotations first.

1 *A vivid image*

'Ah, but a man's reach should exceed his grasp,
Or what's a heaven for?'
Robert Browning (famous poet)

Think about this! You have a picture in your mind (an *image*) of an arm stretching out, reaching for something. But the fingers can't get round it to get a hold of it. ('reach' and 'grasp') And this reaching out after things we can't get a hold of—that's what a heaven is for. Note that he says '*a* heaven', not Heaven with a capital.

2 *An antithetical statement*

'An acre in Middlesex is better than a principality in Utopia.'
Lord Macaulay (famous historian)

This is a well-balanced statement! Lord Macaulay compares a small area, 'acre', with a large area, 'principality' ruled by a prince, and the real world, 'Middlesex', with the *ideal* world of Utopia. Perhaps it is the fact that Middlesex is in England that is of key importance?

What does 'is better than' really mean? 'Better' to whom?

Talking

What is an ideal?
Do you think pursuing an ideal is worthwhile?
If you do, what are the benefits?
If you don't, what do you see as the dangers of being an idealist?
(Note, for example, that the first two idealists you are about to study, Martin Luther King and Abraham Lincoln, were both assassinated. Just coincidence?)

I Have a Dream

by Dr Martin Luther King

"I say to you today even though we face the difficulties of today and tomorrow, I still have a dream. It is a dream that is deeply rooted in the American dream. I have a dream that one day this nation will rise up and live out the true meaning of its creed; 'We hold these truths to be self-evident, that all men are created equal.'

I have a dream that one day on the red hills of Georgia the sons of former slaves and the sons of former slave-owners will be able to sit down together at the table of brotherhood. I have a dream that one day even the state of Mississippi will be transformed into an oasis of freedom and justice.

I have a dream that my four little children one day will live in a nation where they will not be judged by the colour of their skin, but by the content of their character.

This will be the day when all of God's children will be able to sing with new meaning 'Let Freedom Ring'. So let freedom ring from the prodigious hilltops of New Hampshire, let freedom ring from the mighty mountains of New York. But not only that. Let freedom ring from every hill and molehill of Mississippi, from every mountainside. When we allow freedom to ring from every town and every hamlet, from every state and every city, we will be able to speed up that day when all God's children, black men and white men, Jews and Gentiles, Protestants and Catholics, will be able to join hands and sing in the words of the old Negro spiritual, 'Free at last! Free at last! Great God Almighty, we are free at last!'"

There are two events in American history we should all know about:

1 The American colonies breaking away from Britain in the eighteenth century, declaring their independence. (Fourth of July)
2 The Civil War fought in the nineteenth century to abolish slavery. (Gone with the Wind)

Both produced famous idealistic statements of how the Americans saw themselves as a nation.
Read Lincoln's speech, *The Gettysburg Address*, then answer the questions that follow.

The Gettysburg Address

by Abraham Lincoln

Fourscore and seven years ago our fathers brought forth upon this continent a new nation, conceived in liberty, and dedicated to the proposition that all men are created equal. Now we are engaged in a great civil war, testing whether that nation so conceived and so dedicated, can long endure. We are met on a great battlefield of that war. We have come to dedicate a portion of that field as a final resting-place of those who here gave their lives that that nation might live. It is altogether fitting and proper that we should do this. But in a larger sense we cannot dedicate, we cannot consecrate, we cannot hallow this ground. The brave men, living and dead,

who struggled here, have consecrated it far above our power to add or detract. The world will little note, nor long remember, what we say here, but it can never forget what they did here. It is for us, the living, rather to be dedicated here to the unfinished work they have thus far so nobly advanced. It is rather for us to be here dedicated to the great task remaining before us, that from these honoured dead we take increased devotion to that cause for which they here gave the last full measure of devotion; that we here highly resolve that the dead shall not have died in vain, that this nation, under God, shall have a new birth of freedom; and that government of the people, by the people, and for the people, shall not perish from the earth.

(From *Speeches and Letters*, 1907, by Abraham Lincoln.
Address at Dedication of National Cemetery at Gettysburg, 19 November, 1863.)

Reading

The questions are arranged in four sections — and they get harder as you go on.

Section One

1 Complete the following statements.
Lincoln's speech was made in the year .... He delivered this speech at .... where a .... had recently taken place. In his first sentence he refers to an earlier event which occurred .... years before. This event was the famous .... which was made in ....

2 Martin Luther King, in paragraph one of *I Had a Dream*, quotes from this earlier statement. Can you find it and quote it?

3 Explain in your own words what it means.

4 Quote *four* words or phrases from the opening sentence of Lincoln's speech that tie up with the idea of a nation *being born*.

5 What official job was Lincoln at Gettysburg to perform?

Section Two

Here are *nine* sentences. Each one makes a statement, in different words, that is also made by Lincoln. They are all jumbled up and out of order. Write them out in their correct order, as they appear in Lincoln's speech.
(Print the letter clearly at the start of each statement.)

A Many years ago, our nation was begun, founded on the ideal of human equality.
B The men who fought and died here have, by their sacrifice, already done so.
C We have come here today to dedicate a part of this field of conflict as a graveyard.
D Our words today will soon be forgotten: their deeds won't be.
E The Civil War going on at this moment will decide whether that ideal can survive.
F Indeed, it is more fitting that we should dedicate ourselves to complete the task they have begun and died for.
G But in a way we cannot really proclaim that this is holy ground.
H And so, indeed, we should.
I We must determine to renew the democratic ideals of our nation.

Section Three

1 Explain clearly how the contexts help you to arrive at the meanings of 'hallow' and 'detract'.

2 Give fully, and in your own words, what these expressions mean:
  a) 'in a larger sense',
  b) 'little note',
  c) 'highly resolve'.

3 From a book, film or TV programme, draw attention to some aspect of American life that still seems to you to fall short of Lincoln's idealism.

Section Four

Rhetoric is the theory and practice of oratory. Famous orators like Lincoln and Martin Luther King use devices, or tricks, to help them get their messages across.

Climax: arranging words and phrases in order of increasing impact, building up to a peak.
Repetition: repeating a statement or pattern of a statement.
Antithesis: thoughts, words, balanced in contrast.

They try to secure the audience's attention with the impact of their opening, and try to build up to a *peroration*, a rhetorical conclusion, ending with a bang.

They make *direct appeals* to the audience — to the *emotions*, to their *commonsense* and to their *conventions*.

That's quite a lot to take in!
Try to quote and identify any *five* of these devices in Martin Luther King's *I Had a Dream* and *five* from Lincoln's speech, *The Gettysburg Address*.

For a' that, and a' that

by Robert Burns

Is there, for honest Poverty
  That hangs his head, and a' that;
The coward-slave, we pass him by,
  We dare be poor for a' that!
For a' that, and a' that,
  Our toils obscure, and a' that,
The rank is but the guinea's stamp,
  The Man's the gowd for a' that! (*gold*)

What though on hamely fare we dine, (*homely*)
  Wear hoddin grey, and a' that.
Gie fools their silks, and knaves their wine,
  A Man's a Man for a' that.
For a' that, and a' that,
  Their tinsel show, and a' that;
The honest man, though e'er sae poor, (*ever so*)
  Is king o' men for a' that!

Ye see yon birkie ca'd, a lord,
  Wha struts, and stares, and a' that,
Though hundreds worship at his word,
  He's but a coof for a' that.
For a' that, and a' that,
  His riband, star and a' that, (*ribbon*)
The man of independent mind,
  He looks and laughs at a' that!

A prince can mak a belted knight,
  A marquis, duke, and a' that;
But an honest man's aboon his might, (*above*)
  Gude faith he mauna fa' that! (*may not*)
For a' that, and a' that,
  Their dignities, and a' that,
The pith o' Sense, and pride o' Worth,
  Are higher rank than a' that.

Then let us pray that come it may,
  As come it will for a' that,
That Sense and Worth, o'er a' the earth
  Shall bear the gree, and a' that.
For a' that, and a' that,
  It's comin yet for a' that,
That Man to Man the warld o'er,
  Shall brothers be for a' that!

Reading

Look carefully at the poem by Robert Burns. What you will discover is that Burns' ideal *grows out of what he sees wrong in the world about him.* We could sum up the poem like this:

It is clear that Burns reacted to what he saw as the injustice of judging people according to social position and wealth. Ideally, he wanted to see men valued according to their worth, visualising, in place of the divisiveness of rich and poor, high and low, a great future brotherhood of man.

Look back to the speech by Martin Luther King and try to write a similar summing up of *I Had a Dream.*

Read the following short poem by the eighteenth century poet, William Blake, usually called *Jerusalem.* See if you can in a similar way, sum it up.

Jerusalem

by William Blake

And did those feet in ancient time
Walk upon England's mountains green?
And was the holy Lamb of God
On England's pleasant pastures seen?

And did the Countenance Divine
Shine forth upon our clouded hills?
And was Jerusalem builded here,
Among these dark Satanic mills?

Bring me my bow of burning gold:
Bring me my arrows of desire:
Bring me my spear: O clouds unfold!
Bring me my chariot of fire!

I will not cease from mental fight,
Nor shall my sword sleep in my hand,
Till we have built Jerusalem
In England's green & pleasant land.

The Olympic Ideal

by Richard Stilgoe

He stood on one leg and shook the other. He ran gently on the spot. It was cold and very high. HOTLEGS RICARDI, the Italians' white hope for the 1500 metres, looked round the Andorra Olympic stadium. Behind him the band played 'God Save the Queen' as another British hope mounted the winner's rostrum. Across the stadium he saw a Russian lady shot-putter zipping up her flies as she emerged from the Gents.

Andorra had not wanted the Olympic Games, but as the only country who had offended nobody at all for a decade or more, it was inevitable that Andorra would get the Olympic Games. In a desperate attempt to avoid the crippling cost, Andorra tried to gain the world's disapproval by invading Spain. At the orders of the Andorran government the Andorran army marched across the border in broad daylight. But when after three days of occupying Spain even the local Spanish papers had made no mention of its presence, the army went back to Andorra and apologised to the Andorran government, who said it was all right and he had done his best and he could go home now. So the Andorran army went home and started to draw up plans for the stadium, because he was also the Minister of Works.

The games had gone quite well, considering, apart from the marathon. Andorra was not big enough to hold the whole marathon course, which had had to include a loop into France and back. France had been very unco-operative about this, and the marathon times had as a result been very disappointing—as indeed they were bound to be in a race containing two passport checks and a body-search. The 1500 metres was safe within the stadium, though, and hopes of a new world record were high. They rested mainly on the man who stood shaking his arms and legs in the chill mountain air. The world's sports fans had taken to their hearts Hotlegs Ricardi, a child of the slums of Naples, and a gift for the sub-editor because he read meters.

He worked for the Neapolitan Electricity Company, and trained as he made his rounds. Down the basement stairs he ran, through the passages that smelt of oil, past the dumpy ladies in their black dresses, past the pasta hanging on the chair to dry, raise the torch, read the meter, make a note, run back up the basement stairs, run next door, into the church door, crossing himself, run down into the crypt, past the strange plastic limbs put there to remind the Almighty which bits of his flock needed attention (Mamma Ricardi had put two legs in the cabinet last week to make sure the Father ran by his side in the race), into the cupboard beside the crypt, raise the torch, read the figures, write them down, keep running on the spot, running, running. The British papers said he trained for the 1500 metres by doing 120 meters a day. He did not understand the British press. But they showed a picture of him in his running clothes writing down the meter reading at the Napoli stadium. He had only once run at the Napoli stadium, once. Against the clock. Three minutes twenty-nine seconds, they had said. He did not know whether that was fast. They said it was. Today he would find out. Today he ran not against the clock, but against other men, in the Olympics. He had never done this before. There had not been time. They had not let him. Six days he read his meters and ran through Naples. The seventh day was Mass and looking after Mamma. Today he would find out if he was a fast runner, or just a meter-reader from Naples.

The others were taking off their track-suits now. He removed the donkey jacket and threw it aside, the legend 'Electricita Napolitana' gleaming orange on its back.

They lined up. The men in the camel-hair coats who trained the team had told him to let the others lead. He had the big sprint finish, they said. Stay behind the others, stay out of trouble. Then on the third lap . . . !

The gun surprised him, and he found he had no choice but to obey their orders. He *was* behind the others, but only a little, and it was easy to keep up. They did not, he thought, go very fast. He ran steadily, maybe five metres behind the pack, watching their numbered backs moving up and down.

After one lap he still felt fine.

After two laps he was bored. This was very easy. He had no need to worry. The pack ran on in front.

At the beginning of the final lap they rang a bell, a bell just like a doorbell, the sort of doorbell he rang all day. Why did they ring the bell? What was he doing here? He was running. The 1500 metres. He would never manage 1500 meters. He must hurry. Not pausing for a second, Hotlegs Ricardi made his decision; he stopped, grabbed a clipboard from a track official and calmly copied down all the numbers from the backs of the disappearing runners.

(From *The Richard Stilgoe Letters*)

Symbol

A symbol is an emblem, something that by custom and convention, comes to represent something else.
A familiar symbol is this —

— that's right! The Olympic symbol.

Ideally, we know that the Olympic Games should bring the peoples of the world together, in friendly and individual competition. It is all about taking part, not winning.... and so on.
Can you explain how this symbol represents something of this ideal?
Why five circles and why linked the way they are?

Talking

In small groups, perhaps, list *eight* aspects of modern Olympiads that seem to deny the spirit of Olympic idealism. Try, wherever possible, to quote specific examples of failure.

Reading

Questions on Richard Stilgoe's *The Olympic Ideal.*

1 Hotlegs Ricardi — you may not have noticed it, but this is an *anagram* of the writer's name. What, therefore, is an anagram?

2 Explain why sometimes the spelling is *meters* and sometimes *metres*.

3 What use has the writer made of this confusion?

4 Why, according to the writer, did the *authorities* decide to hold the Games in Andorra?

5 Why, in your view, did the *writer* himself pick on Andorra?

6 Quote the expression that shows why the Andorrans didn't want to hold the Games. What does this mean?

7 What did they do to try to avoid being hosts to the Olympics?

8 What was the result of their action?

9 Look up these words in the dictionary. *Ironic, Whimsical, Sarcastic.* Which word best defines the tone of the comment on the Marathon?

10 What does a sub-editor on a newspaper do? Explain why the writer says, 'a gift for the sub-editor because he read meters'?

11 Explain in your own words:
   a) why you think Hotlegs could have won the 1500 metres?
   b) why he didn't?
   c) whether, in not winning, he actually justified the title — *The Olympic Ideal?*

12 When we say that something we read 'is funny', makes us laugh, smile, etc. — we can mean many different things. It was amusing, witty, comic, farcical, side-splitting, absurd, ridiculous, satirical, hilarious, and so on.
   Choose from Richard Stilgoe's Letter *five* examples of things you found 'funny'. They might be incidents or expressions, the way he says it, etc. Indicate clearly what the five are, say what type of humour they are, and how you reacted to them.
   (You can, if you wish, point to something he obviously meant to be funny, that you didn't find funny at all. Try to explain why.)

An extract from the *Universal Declaration of Human Rights 1948*

Civil and political rights

3 Everyone has the right to life, liberty and security of person.

4 No one shall be held in slavery or servitude; . . .

5 No one shall be subjected to torture or to cruel, inhuman or degrading treatment or punishment.

6 Everyone has the right to recognition everywhere as a person before the law.

7 All are equal before the law . . . .

8 Everyone has the right to an effective remedy by the competent national tribunals for acts violating the fundamental rights granted him by the constitution or by law.

9 No one shall be subjected to arbitrary arrest, detention or exile.

10 Everyone is entitled in full equality to a fair and public hearing by an independent and impartial tribunal . . .

11 Everyone charged with a penal offence has the right to be presumed innocent until proved guilty . . .

12 No one shall be subjected to arbitrary interference with his privacy, family, home or correspondence, nor to attacks upon his honour and reputation . . . .

13 Everyone has the right to freedom of movement and residence within the borders of each State.

Everyone has the right to leave any country, including his own, and to return to his country.

14 Everyone has the right to seek and to enjoy in other countries asylum from persecution . . . .

15 Everyone has the right to a nationality . . . .

16 Men and women of full age . . . have the right to marry and to found a family. They are entitled to equal rights as to marriage, during marriage and at its dissolution . . . .

17 Everyone has the right to own property alone as well as in association with others.

No one shall be arbitrarily deprived of his property.

18 Everyone has the right to freedom of thought, conscience and religion; . . .

19 Everyone has the right to freedom of opinion and expression; . . .

20 Everyone has the right to freedom of peaceful assembly and association.
No one may be compelled to belong to an association.

21 Everyone has the right to take part in the government of his country, directly or through freely chosen representatives . . .

Economic, social and cultural rights

22 Everyone, as a member of society, has the right to social security.

23 Everyone has the right to work.
Everyone has the right to equal pay for equal work.
Everyone who works has the right to just and favourable remuneration.
Everyone has the right to form and to join trade unions for the protection of his interests.

24 Everyone has the right to rest and leisure . . . .

25 Everyone has the right to a standard of living adequate for the health and well-being of himself and of his family . . . .
Motherhood and childhood are entitled to special care and assistance. All children, whether born in or out of wedlock, shall enjoy the same social protection.

26 Everyone has the right to education. Education shall be free, at least in the elementary and fundamental stages. Elementary education shall be compulsory.

27 Everyone has the right freely to participate in the cultural life of the community . . . .
Everyone has the right to the protection of the moral and material interests resulting from any scientific, literary or artistic production of which he is the author.

28 Everyone is entitled to a social and international order in which the rights and freedoms set forth in this Declaration can be fully realised.

Reading

1 Explain, in your own words, and by example if you wish, what you understand by paragraphs 8 and 27.

2 Choose *three* paragraphs from the Section on Civil and Political Rights setting out ideals from this Declaration.
Comment on how far in your opinion each one is observed in:
a) the United Kingdom
b) any other part of the world.

My Blue Heaven
(Pop-song, 1927)

When whip poorwills call
and ev'ning is nigh,
I hurry to my blue heaven.
A turn to the right,
a little white light,
Will lead you to my blue heaven.

You'll see a smiling face, a fireplace,
a cosy room,
A little nest that's nestled where
the roses bloom.

Just Mollie and me,
And Baby makes three,
We're happy in my blue heaven.

(Words by George Whiting, music by Walter Donaldson)

Reading

Read the words of the 'pop' song, *My Blue Heaven.*

1 Why is the heaven a 'blue' heaven?

2 List all the ingredients of the writer's heaven, underlining all those words that seem to you to stress either the idea of 'small' or the idea of 'cosy'.

3 What conclusions would you draw about the nature of the writer's idealism?

4 Note the date ot *My Blue Heaven*, 1927 was the time of the Depression, unemployment and severe hardships. To what extent, in your opinion, could that 'dream' of the song be linked to its period in history?

Extract from *Of Mice and Men*

by John Steinbeck

George and the powerful but simple-minded Lennie have arrived at a ranch to work as casual labourers. It's a dull and boring routine. What keeps them going is a shared dream. Although Lennie has learned all about their dream place *by heart,* he still likes George to tell him all about it. . .time after time.

Lennie said, 'Tell about that place, George.'

'I jus' tol' you jus' las' night.'

'Go on—tell again, George.'

'Well, it's ten acres,' said George. 'Got a little win'mill. Got a little shack on it, an' a chicken run. Got a kitchen, orchard cherries, apples, peaches, 'cots, nuts, got a few berries. They's a place for alfalfa and plenty water to flood it. They's a pig pen.'

'An' rabbits, George.'

'No place for rabbits now, but I could easy build a few hutches and you could feed alfalfa to the rabbits.'

'Damn right, I could,' said Lennie. 'You god-damn right I could.'

George's hands stopped working with the cards. His voice was growing warmer. 'An' we could have a few pigs. I could build a smoke-house like the one gran'pa had, an' when we kill a pig we can smoke the bacon and the hams, and make sausage an' all like that. An' when the salmon run up the river we could catch a hundred of 'em an' salt 'em down or smoke 'em. We could have them for breakfast. They ain't nothing so nice as smoked salmon. When the fruit come in we could can it—and tomatoes, they're easy to can. Ever' Sunday we'd kill a chicken or a rabbit. Maybe, we'd have a cow or a goat, and the cream is so goddamn thick you got to cut it with a knife and take it out with a spoon.'

Lennie watched him with wide eyes, and old Candy watched him too. Lennie said softly, 'We could live offa the fatta the lan'.'

'Sure,' said George. 'All kin's a vegetables in the garden, and if we want a little whisky we can sell a few eggs or something, or some milk. We'd jus' live there. We'd belong there. There wouldn't be no more runnin' round the country and gettin' fed by a Jap cook. No, sir, we'd have our own place where we belonged and not sleep in no bunk-house.'

'Tell about the house, George,' Lennie begged.

'Sure, we'd have a little house an' a room to ourself. Little fat iron stove, an' in the winter we'd keep a fire goin' in it. It ain't enough land so we'd have to work too hard. Maybe six, seven hours a day. We wouldn't have to buck no barley eleven hours a day. An' when we put in a crop, why, we'd be there to take the crop up. We'd know what come of our planting.'

'An' rabbits,' Lennie said eagerly. 'An' I'd take care of 'em. Tell how I'd do that, George.'

'Sure, you'd go out in the alfalfa patch an' you'd have a sack. You'd fill up the sack and bring it in an' put in the rabbit cages.'

'They'd nibble an' they'd nibble,' said Lennie, 'the way they do. I seen 'em.'

'Ever' six weeks or so,' George continued, 'them does would throw a litter, so we'd have plenty rabbits to eat an' to sell. An' we'd keep a few pigeons to go flyin' around the win'mill like they done when I was a kid.' He looked raptly at the wall over Lennie's head. 'An' it'd be our own, an' nobody could can us. If we don't like a guy we can say, "Get the hell out," and by God he's got to do it. An' if a fren' come along, why we'd have an extra bunk, and we'd say, "Why don't you spen' the night?" an' by God he would. We'd have a setter dog and a couple stripe cats, but you gotta watch out them cats don't get the little rabbits.'

Lennie breathed hard. 'You jus' let 'em try to get the rabbits. I'll break their god-damn necks. I'll . . . I'll smash 'em with a stick.' He subsided, grumbling to himself, threatening the future cats which might dare to disturb the future rabbits.

George sat entranced with his own picture.

Reading

1 Look at this sequence:
   a) 'I jus' tol' you jus' las' night.'
   b) George's hands stopped working with the cards. His voice was growing warmer.
   c) He looked raptly at the wall over Lennie's head.
   d) George sat entranced with his own picture.

   What does this tell you about George as he is telling the dream to Lennie?

2 Examine carefully the ways in which Lennie, although he is meant to be simple-minded, manages to keep George going.

3 List the details that make up the dream, under the following headings:
   the land,
   the livestock,
   the house itself,
   becoming independent,
   lifestyle.

   Study the itemised details carefully. Perhaps you think that they are not asking much — rather simple things. What comments would you offer on the *quality* of George and Lennie's ideal?

Writing

1 When you get older, and have all sorts of problems like mortgages, bills, car repairs, children to feed, etc., you tend to be more preoccupied with the harsh realities of making sure that two plus two equals four at the end of the month. Idealism seems a luxury. That's why so many people feel that the time to be full of ideals is when you are young.

Using the following quotation as your title, discuss whether you think that this is true.
'Modern medical opinion is of the mind that youth is the best time to catch idealism — like mumps, measles or chickenpox.'

2 A totally uninhabited island has been left to you by a deceased uncle. You wish to found a small community on this island. What sort of people would you be trying to recruit? What principles would govern life and attitudes on this idyllic isle? How would things be run? How would you *live*?
Or
To what extent do you think that people who lead the religious life, say in a monastery or convent, lead an *ideal* existence? In terms of your ideals? In terms of theirs?

3 'Dreams and ideals are often concerned with basic things — but these basics are what are required for *human dignity* and the *peaceful co-existence of mankind.'*
Referring to any of the texts studied, discuss whether you think this is true.

Reading (Literature)

1 Re-read the speeches by Martin Luther King and Lincoln. Which do you find more persuasive? Give reasons for your choice.

2 'Idealistic poems tend to be more idealistic than poems.'
Is this true? Discuss the *poetic* merits, what makes it good poetry of either of the two poems read, or of any other 'ideal world' poem you have read.

3 By a close examination of one of the two pop songs in this unit, or both of them, discuss whether you think the words of a pop song can be taken seriously *as poetry*, basing your discussion on *My Blue Heaven*.

Find out what Amnesty International does. When you have done so, in a short paragraph, discuss the appositeness of this organisation's symbol.

It is *people* who have such dreams — perhaps because we *need* them.
It is *people* who make sure that such dreams never become *reality*.

This is the subject of the following units.

The symbol of
Amnesty International.

Unit 2

Getting in the Way

PREJUDICE

Prejudice — 'pre-judge'. Means a judgement or opinion formed beforehand, without due examination.

To be prejudiced — to hold such opinions, usually unfavourable ones, without due examination.

Put like that, it sounds a bit silly to be prejudiced: to hold opinions about things you haven't found out about, or people you don't know. Why do so many people do such an apparently silly thing, why do perhaps all of us do it to some extent?

Classical Music	Its snobby.
Egg sandwiches	Don't like the taste!
Poetry	Boring and old fashioned.
Cricket	Boring! I never watch it.
Chinese Food	Don't like the taste.
English people	Speak with snob accents.
Maths	Too hard and lots of homework
Girls	Because they are girls and soppy.
Curry	Smells
Royal Family	Agree with dad. Get rid of them all!

Look at the list above.

a) How much can you deduce about the person who wrote it?

b) How many of the writer's dislikes would you class as prejudices?

c) What are your reasons for saying that these are prejudices?

d) Can you work out a way of testing whether something is a prejudice or not?

e) How would you go about it?

By the way, do you think that the person who completed this has, without meaning to, told us a lot *about himself*? What do you think he has betrayed?

Now read the following short passage carefully.

Extract from *The Knife* by Judah Waten

'Cop the cheeky dago,' one of her companions said.

It was Tommy Lawler, a tall, strong, good-looking youth of nineteen who wore an open-necked Hawaiian style shirt and a two-toned coat, almost reaching down to his knees. The girl, Mavis Keer, laughed and stared back at Plinio until he disappeared round the corner into his street.

'I can't stick dagos,' Tommy went on rancorously.

His companions were well aware of his dislike. He was just like his father with whom he worked at the Victoria Market. Old Lawler never tired of saying that dagos could live on the smell of an oil rag; that way back in the depression when returned soldiers were forced off their farms, they had taken them over, and in the cities they had taken the jobs of Australians.

Young Tommy repeated his father's words as if they were holy writ. But until Plinio had appeared on the scene he had not railed against any particular Italian, but Italians in general. Now he began to fasten all his antipathy on this olive-skinned youth in the cap and dark corduroy trousers.

Reading

1 Express 'cop the dago' in more formal English.

2 What is the 'dago' called?

3 a) What caused Tommy's comment in the first line?
b) What evidence in the passage supports this?

4 What does 'rancorously' mean?

5 a) 'His companions were well aware of his dislike.'
What does this statement tell you about Tommy?
b) Where do Tommy's views on Italians come from?
c) In your own words, explain how this attitude started in the first place.

6 'Young Tommy repeated his father's words as if they were holy writ.'
Explain what this means.

7 'Until Plinio had appeared on the scene he had not railed against any particular Italian, but Italians in general.'
a) What does 'railed' mean?
b) What does it suggest about Tommy's contact with Italians till that time?

Talking

1 If Tommy *liked* Italians without ever having met one, just because his father liked them, would that be wrong?

2 Is Tommy wrong to accept what his father says unquestioningly?
Should we take nothing on trust, not accept any view until we have examined it and satisfied ourselves that it is correct?

Human beings tend to be a bit afraid, apprehensive of anything new, strange, different. In some cultures, however, welcoming strangers is a point of honour. Anyone failing to show respect, hospitality to a stranger brings disgrace on himself and his society. But in other cultures, strangers are viewed with suspicion and hostility: they may even be killed (and in some cases, eaten). The fear of strangers, hatred of foreigners, is called *xenophobia*, and much prejudice has its origins here.

Chinese Puzzle

Extract from *Typhoon*

by Joseph Conrad

This Chinaman here was coming with the ship as far as Fu-chau — a sort of interpreter he would be. Bun Hin's clerk he was, and wanted to have a look at the space. Jukes had better take him forward. "D'ye hear, Jukes?"

Jukes took care to punctuate these instructions in proper places with the obligatory "Yes, sir," ejaculated without enthusiasm. His brusque "Come along, John; make look see" set the Chinaman in motion at his heels.

"Wanchee look see, all same look see can do," said Jukes, who having no talent for foreign languages mangled the very pidgin-English* cruelly. He pointed at the open hatch. "Catchee number one piecie place to sleep in. Eh?"

He was gruff, as became his racial superiority, but not unfriendly. The Chinaman, gazing sad and speechless into the darkness of the hatchway, seemed to stand at the head of a yawning grave.

"No catchee rain down there—savee?" pointed out Jukes. "Suppose all'ee same fine weather, one piecie coolie-man come topside," he pursued, warming up imaginatively. "Make so—Phooooo!" He expanded his chest and blew out his cheeks. "Savee, John? Breathe—fresh air. Good. Eh? Washee him piecie pants, chow-chow topside—see, John?"

With his mouth and hands he made exuberant motions of eating rice and washing clothes; and the Chinaman who concealed his distrust of this pantomime under a collected demeanour tinged by a gentle and refined melancholy, glanced out of his almond eyes from Jukes to the hatch and back again. "Velly good," he murmured, in a disconsolate undertone, and hastened smoothly along the decks, dodging obstacles in his course. He disappeared, ducking low under a sling of ten dirty gunny-bags full of some costly merchandise and exhaling a repulsive smell.

* Pidgin English: 'pidgin' is a Chinese corruption of the English word 'business'. Pidgin English is, strictly speaking, a jargon consisting mainly of English words in a Chinese arrangement, used in communication between Chinese and foreigners. Also used, loosely, for English and another language.

Reading

1 Try to translate Jukes' pidgin English into standard English.

2 'He was gruff, as became his racial superiority, but not unfriendly.' It is clear that Jukes believes in his superiority, that the Chinese are somehow 'inferior'.
By studying the passage as a whole, try to work out:
a) in what ways Jukes considers the Chinese to be inferior,
b) whether you think the writer, Conrad, perhaps shares Jukes' opinion.

Talking

'An Englishman in Italy is a friend; a European in China; and perhaps a man would be beloved as such, were we to meet him on the moon.'

(David Hume, the philosopher)

a) What point is Hume making here?
b) How does it fit in with our discussion of prejudice?

A 14-year old boy, who might well grow up to be a philosopher himself one day, wrote in an essay—

'It's the easiest trick in the book! Stick somebody you don't like in a group—colour, religion, mod, rocker, swot, race, accent—so you can tie a label round his neck. And you've got him!'

The easiest trick! I wonder.

Be absolutely honest about this.

1 What groups can you distinguish in your own age group?

2 Name *three* of these groups. What are the distinguishing features of these three groups?

3 Is there any ground for classing one of these groups as *either* inferior *or* superior to the other two?

4 Which group do you belong to?

5 If one member of a group wronged you, would you be justified in blaming all the members of that group?

6 If a member of your group — classmate, team-mate, fellow-countryman — achieves something, are you entitled to a share of the glory?

Here are two extracts taken from *The Merchant of Venice* by Shakespeare. Shylock is a Jewish moneylender. In the first extract he has just been approached by Antonio, a wealthy Venetian merchant, who wishes to borrow a large sum of money as he is a bit short of the 'readies'.

Extracts from *The Merchant of Venice*
by William Shakespeare

Antonio. Well, Shylock, shall we be beholding to you?

Shylock. Signior Antonio, many a time and oft
In the Rialto you have rated me
About my moneys and my usances.
Still have I borne it with a patient shrug,
For suff'rance is the badge of all our tribe.
You call me misbeliever, cutthroat dog,
And spet upon my Jewish gaberdine,
And all for use of that which is mine own.
Well then, it now appears you need my help.
Go to, then. You come to me and you say,
"Shylock, we would have moneys"—you say so,
You that did void your rheum upon my beard
And foot me as you spurn a stranger cur
Over your threshold! Moneys is your suit.
What should I say to you? Should I not say,
"Hath a dog money? Is it possible
A cur can lend three thousand ducats?" Or
Shall I bend low, and in a bondman's key,
With bated breath, and whisp'ring humbleness,
Say this:

"Fair sir, you spet on me on Wednesday last,
You spurned me such a day, another time
You called me dog; and for these courtesies
I'll lend you thus much moneys?"

Antonio. I am as like to call thee so again,
To spet on thee again, to spurn thee too.

In the second extract, Antonio's business has failed and he is unable to repay the loan, so that Shylock is entitled to claim his surety, his guarantee, which was a pound of Antonio's flesh.

Salerio. Why, I am sure if he forfeit thou wilt not take his flesh. What's that good for?

Shylock. To bait fish withal. If it will feed nothing else, it will feed my revenge. He hath disgraced me, and hind'red me half a million, laughed at my losses, mocked at my gains, scorned my nation, thwarted my bargains, cooled my friends, heated mine enemies—and what's his reason? I am a Jew. Hath not a

Jew eyes? Hath not a Jew hands, organs, dimensions, senses, affections, passions —fed with the same food, hurt with the same weapons, subject to the same diseases, healed by the same means, warmed and cooled by the same winter and summer as a Christian is? If you prick us, do we not bleed? If you tickle us, do we not laugh? If you poison us, do we not die? And if you wrong us, shall we not revenge? If we are like you in the rest, we will resemble you in that. If a Jew wrong a Christian, what is his humility? Revenge! If a Christian wrong a Jew, what should his sufferance be by Christian example? Why revenge! The villainy you teach me I will execute, and it shall go hard but I will better the instruction.

Reading

1 In Unit 1 you came across the rhetorical device of *climax*. Quote from Shylock's first speech a good example of this.

2 Another rhetorical device is the *rhetorical question*. Here, the speaker turns a statement into a question. This can be very effective. For example, 'A dog has no money' is not nearly as powerful as 'Hath a dog money?'
   a) Write down *four* rhetorical questions from the second speech, then re-write these as statements.
   b) Do you think they are less effective as statements? If so, try to give a reason why this is so.

3 Under the Nazis, the yellow star of David was the 'badge' of the Jews. What 'badge' does Shylock claim the Jews have to wear? What does he mean by this?

4 Explain what the following mean:
   a) 'void your rheum upon my beard',
   b) 'Moneys is your suit.'

5 Look carefully at the four lines in inverted commas at the conclusion of Shylock's first speech.
   a) How does he tell us, in your own words, how these lines should be read?
   b) What should be the tone of this speech?
   c) Why does he refer to his treatment by Antonio as 'courtesies'?

6 Write down *two* headings — For Shylock and Against Shylock.
On the basis of what you've learned in the two speeches, list all the evidence you can muster *for* and *against*.
Whose side are you on? Give reasons.
Whose side do you think Shakespeare was on? Give reasons.

7 Read the last few lines of Shylock's second speech, from 'And if you wrong us....'
If a Christian treats a man badly because he is a Jew, can the Christian complain if the Jew treats him badly because he is a Christian?
In terms of prejudice, what would be the consequence?

The Test

by Angelica Gibbs

On the afternoon Marian took her second driver's test, Mrs. Ericson went with her. 'It's probably better to have someone a little older with you,' Mrs. Ericson said as Marian slipped into the driver's seat beside her. 'Perhaps the last time your Cousin Bill made you nervous, talking too much on the way.'

'Yes, Ma'am,' Marian said in her soft unaccented voice. 'They probably do like it better if a white person shows up with you.'

'Oh, I don't think it's *that*,' Mrs. Ericson began, and subsided after a glance at the girl's set profile. Marian drove the car slowly through the shady suburban streets. It was one of the first hot days in June, and when they reached the boulevard they found it crowded with cars headed for the beaches.

'Do you want me to drive?' Mrs. Ericson asked. 'I'll be glad to if you're feeling jumpy.' Marian shook her head. Mrs. Ericson watched her dark, competent hands and wondered for the thousandth time how the house had ever managed to get along without her, or how she had lived through those earlier years when her household had been presided over by a series of slatternly white girls who had considered housework demeaning and the care of children an added insult. 'You drive beautifully, Marian,' she said. 'Now, don't think of the last time. Anybody would slide on a steep hill on a wet day like that.'

'It takes four mistakes to flunk you,' Marian said. 'I don't remember doing all the things the inspector marked down on my blank.'

'People say that they only want you to slip them a little something,' Mrs. Ericson said doubtfully.

'*No*,' Marian said. 'That would only make it worse, Mrs. Ericson, I know.'

The car turned right, at a traffic signal, into a side road and slid up to the curb at the rear of a short line of parked cars. The inspectors had not arrived yet.

'You have the papers?' Mrs. Ericson asked. Marian took them out of her bag: her learner's permit, the car registration, and her birth certificate. They settled down to the dreary business of waiting.

'It will be marvellous to have someone dependable to drive the children to school every day,' Mrs. Ericson said.

Marian looked up from the list of driving requirements she had been studying. 'It'll make things simpler at the house, won't it?' she said.

'Oh, Marian,' Mrs. Ericson exclaimed, 'if I could only pay you half of what you're worth!'

'Now, Mrs. Ericson,' Marian said firmly. They looked at each other and smiled with affection.

Two cars with official insignia on their doors stopped across the street. The inspectors leaped out, very brisk and military in their neat uniforms. Marian's hands tightened on the wheel. 'There's the one who flunked me last time,' she whispered, pointing to a stocky, self-important man who had begun to shout directions at the driver at the head of the line. 'Oh, Mrs. Ericson.'

'Now, Marian,' Mrs. Ericson said. They smiled at each other again, rather weakly.

The inspector who finally reached their car was not the stocky one but a genial, middle-aged man who grinned broadly as he thumbed over their papers. Mrs. Ericson started to get out of the car. 'Don't you want to come along?' the inspector asked. 'Mandy and I don't mind company.'

Mrs. Ericson was bewildered for a moment. 'No,' she said, and stepped to the curb. 'I might make Marian self-conscious. She's a fine driver, Inspector.'

'Sure thing,' the inspector said, winking at Mrs. Ericson. He slid into the seat beside Marian. 'Turn right at the corner, Mandy-Lou.'

From the curb, Mrs. Ericson watched the car move smoothly up the street.

The inspector made notations in a small black book. 'Age?' he inquired presently, as they drove along.

'Twenty-seven'.

He looked at Marian out of the corner of his eye. 'Old enough to have quite a flock of pickaninnies, eh?'

Marian did not answer.

'Left at this corner,' the inspector said, 'and park between that truck and the green Buick.'

The two cars were very close together, but Marian squeezed in between them without too much manoeuvering. 'Driven before, Mandy-Lou?' the inspector asked.

'Yes, sir. I had a license for three years in Pennsylvania.'

'Why do you want to drive a car?'

'My employer needs me to take her children to and from school.'

'Sure you don't really want to sneak out nights to meet some young blood?' the inspector asked. He laughed as Marian shook her head.

'Let's see you take a left at the corner and then turn around in the middle of the next block,' the inspector said. He began to whistle 'Swanee River.' 'Make you homesick?' he asked.

Marian put out her hand, swung around neatly in the street, and headed back in the direction from which they had come. 'No,' she said. 'I was born in Scranton, Pennsylvania.'

The inspector feigned astonishment. 'You-all ain't Southern?' he said. 'Well, dog my cats if I didn't think you-all came from down yondah.'

'No, sir,' Marian said.

'Turn onto Main Street and let's see how you-all does in heavier traffic.'

They followed a line of cars along Main Street for several blocks until they came in sight of a concrete bridge which arched high over the railroad tracks.

'Read that sign at the end of the bridge,' the inspector said.

'"Proceed with caution. Dangerous in slippery weather,"' Marian said.

'You-all sho can read fine,' the inspector exclaimed. 'Where d'you learn to do that, Mandy?'

'I got my college degree last year,' Marian said. Her voice was not quite steady.

As the car crept up the slope of the bridge the inspector burst out laughing. He laughed so hard he could scarcely give his next direction. 'Stop here,' he said, wiping his eyes, 'then start 'er up again. Mandy got her degree, did she? Dog my cats!'

Marian pulled up beside the curb. She put the car in neutral, pulled on the emergency, waited a moment, and then put the car into gear again. Her face was set. As she released the brake her foot slipped off the clutch pedal and the engine stalled.

'Now, Mistress Mandy,' the inspector said, 'remember your degree.'

'*Damn* you!' Marian cried. She started the car with a jerk.

The inspector lost his joviality in an instant. 'Return to the starting place, please,' he said, and made four very black crosses at random in the squares on Marian's application blank.

Mrs. Ericson was waiting at the curb where they had left her. As Marian stopped the car, the inspector jumped out and brushed past her, his face purple. 'What happened?' Mrs. Ericson asked, looking after him with alarm.

Marian stared down at the wheel and her lip trembled.

'Oh, Marian, *again*?' Mrs. Ericson said.

Marian nodded. 'In a sort of different way,' she said, and slid over to the right-hand side of the car.

After You, My Dear Alphonse

by Shirley Jackson

Mrs. Wilson was just taking the gingerbread out of the oven when she heard Johnny outside talking to someone.

'Johnny,' she called, 'you're late. Come in and get your lunch.'

'Just a minute, Mother,' Johnny said. 'After you, my dear Alphonse.'

'After *you*, my dear Alphonse,' another voice said.

'No, after *you*, my dear Alphonse,' Johnny said.

Mrs. Wilson opened the door. 'Johnny,' she said, 'you come in this minute and get your lunch. You can play after you've eaten.'

Johnny came in after her, slowly. 'Mother,' he said, 'I brought Boyd home for lunch with me.'

'Boyd?' Mrs. Wilson thought for a moment. 'I don't believe I've met Boyd. Bring him in, dear, since you've invited him. Lunch is ready.'

'Boyd!' Johnny yelled. 'Hey, Boyd, come on in!'

'I'm coming. Just got to unload this stuff.'

'Well, hurry, or my mother'll be sore.'

'Johnny, that's not very polite to either your friend or your mother,' Mrs. Wilson said. 'Come sit down, Boyd.'

As she turned to show Boyd where to sit, she saw he was a Negro boy, smaller than Johnny but about the same age. His arms were loaded with split kindling wood. 'Where'll I put this stuff, Johnny?' he asked.

Mrs. Wilson turned to Johnny. 'Johnny,' she said, 'what did you make Boyd do? What is that wood?'

'Dead Japanese,' Johnny said mildly. 'We stand them in the ground and run over them with tanks.'

'How do you do, Mrs. Wilson?' Boyd said.

'How do you do, Boyd? You shouldn't let Johnny make you carry all that wood. Sit down now and eat lunch, both of you.'

'Why shouldn't he carry the wood, Mother? It's his wood. We got it at his place.'

'Johnny,' Mrs. Wilson said, 'go on and eat your lunch.'

'Sure,' Johnny said. He held out the dish of scrambled eggs to Boyd. 'After you, my dear Alphonse.'

'After *you*, my dear Alphonse,' Boyd said.

'After *you*, my dear Alphonse,' Johnny said. They began to giggle.

'Are you hungry, Boyd?' Mrs. Wilson asked.

'Yes, Mrs. Wilson.'

'Well, don't let Johnny stop you. He always fusses about eating, so you just see that you get a good lunch. There's plenty of food here for you to have all you want.'

'Thank you, Mrs. Wilson.'

'Come on, Alphonse,' Johnny said. He pushed half the scrambled eggs on to Boyd's plate. Boyd watched while Mrs. Wilson put a dish of stewed tomatoes beside his plate.

'Boyd don't eat tomatoes, do you, Boyd?' Johnny said.

'*Doesn't* eat tomatoes, Johnny. And just because you don't like them, don't say that about Boyd. Boyd will eat *anything*.'

'Bet he won't,' Johnny said, attacking his scrambled eggs.

'Boyd wants to grow up and be a big strong man so he can work hard,' Mrs. Wilson said. 'I'll bet Boyd's father eats stewed tomatoes.'

'My father eats anything he wants to,' Boyd said.

'So does mine,' Johnny said. 'Sometimes he doesn't eat hardly anything. He's a little guy, though. Wouldn't hurt a flea.'

'Mine's a little guy, too,' Boyd said.

'I'll bet he's strong, though,' Mrs. Wilson said. She hesitated. 'Does he . . . work?'

'Sure,' Johnny said. 'Boyd's father works in a factory.'

'There, you see?' Mrs. Wilson said. 'And he certainly has to be strong to do that— all that lifting and carrying at a factory.'

'Boyd's father doesn't have to,' Johnny said. 'He's a foreman.'

Mrs. Wilson felt defeated. 'What does your mother do, Boyd?'

'My mother?' Boyd was surprised. 'She takes care of us kids.'

'Oh. She doesn't work, then?'

'Why should she?' Johnny said through a mouthful of eggs. 'You don't work.'

'You really don't want any stewed tomatoes, Boyd?'

'No, thank you, Mrs. Wilson,' Boyd said.

'No, thank you, Mrs. Wilson, no, thank you, Mrs. Wilson, no thank you, Mrs. Wilson,' Johnny said. 'Boyd's sister's going to work, though. She's going to be a teacher.'

'That's a very fine attitude for her to have, Boyd.' Mrs. Wilson restrained an impulse to pat Boyd on the head. 'I imagine you're all very proud of her?'

'I guess so,' Boyd said.

'What about all your other brothers and sisters? I guess all of you want to make just as much of yourselves as you can.'

'There's only me and Jean,' Boyd said. 'I don't know yet what I want to be when I grow up.'

'We're going to be tank drivers, Boyd and me,' Johnny said. 'Zoom.' Mrs. Wilson caught Boyd's glass of milk as Johnny's napkin ring, suddenly transformed into a tank, plowed heavily across the table.

'Look, Johnny,' Boyd said. 'Here's a foxhole. I'm shooting at you.'

Mrs. Wilson, with the speed born of long experience, took the gingerbread off the shelf and placed it carefully between the tank and the foxhole.

'Now eat as much as you want to, Boyd,' she said. 'I want to see you get filled up.'

'Boyd eats a lot, but not as much as I do,' Johnny said. 'I'm bigger than he is.'

'You're not much bigger,' Boyd said. 'I can beat you running.'

Mrs. Wilson took a deep breath. 'Boyd,' she said. Both boys turned to her. 'Boyd, Johnny has some suits that are a little too small for him, and a winter coat. It's not new, of course, but there's lots of wear in it still. And I have a few dresses that your mother or sister could probably use. Your mother can make them into lots of things for all of you, and I'd be very happy to give them to you. Suppose before you leave I make up a big bundle and then you and Johnny can take it over to your mother right away . . .' Her voice trailed off as she saw Boyd's puzzled expression.

'But I have plenty of clothes, thank you,' he said. 'And I don't think my mother knows how to sew very well, and anyway I guess we buy about everything we need. Thank you very much, though.'

'We don't have time to carry that old stuff around, Mother,' Johnny said. 'We got to play tanks with the kids today.'

Mrs. Wilson lifted the plate of gingerbread off the table as Boyd was about to take another piece. 'There are many little boys like you, Boyd, who would be very grateful for the clothes someone was kind enough to give them.'

'Boyd will take them if you want him to, Mother,' Johnny said.

'I didn't mean to make you mad, Mrs. Wilson,' Boyd said.

'Don't think I'm angry, Boyd. I'm just disappointed in you, that's all. Now let's not say anything more about it.'

She began clearing the plates off the table, and Johnny took Boyd's hand and pulled him to the door. "Bye, Mother," Johnny said. Boyd stood for a minute, staring at Mrs. Wilson's back.

'After you, my dear Alphonse,' Johnny said, holding the door open.

'Is your mother still mad?' Mrs. Wilson heard Boyd ask in a low voice.

'I don't know,' Johnny said. 'She's screwy sometimes.'

'So's mine,' Boyd said. He hesitated. 'After *you*, my dear Alphonse.'

Stereotypes: A prejudice often produces a stereotype i.e. a figure supposed to represent all the typical features of a group. In reality it is an embodiment of and focus for all one's prejudices.

Stereotypes can be quite funny — or extremely offensive!

For example:

A stereotype Scot is called Jock, he eats haggis, wears a kilt. Frequently drunk, aggressive — always mean. Says 'Och aye', 'Hoots mon' and 'the noo'.

A stereotype Englishman is called Nigel. Wears a bowler hat, pinstripe trousers and carries a rolled umbrella and brief case. Says 'What ho', 'Jolly good,' and talks incessantly about the weather and cricket.

Reading

1 *The Test*
It is obvious that the examiner in this story is prejudiced about blacks, and has a stereotyped notion of what they are like. By looking closely at what he says and does, build up a detailed picture of what his 'typical' negro girl is like.

2 *After You, My Dear Alphonse*
Mrs Wilson, perhaps a bit less obviously, is attempting to fit Boyd and his family into her stereotyped picture of the negro family. By looking closely at the assumptions she makes, build up a detailed picture of Mrs Wilson's 'typical' black family.

3 Now compare the results. Can you detect any common factors between the two stereotypes?

4 'The main difference is that while Marian is well aware of what is going on, Boyd has no idea why Johnny's mother is asking all these strange questions.' Do you think this is an important point?
Explain clearly in what way you see it as important in a) *The Test* and b) *After You, My Dear Alphonse*.
In your view, is it the *main* difference between the two stories? If you think it is, give a reason. If not, say clearly what you feel the main difference is.

5 *Characterisation*
There is a neat little triangle of characters in each story.

The Test

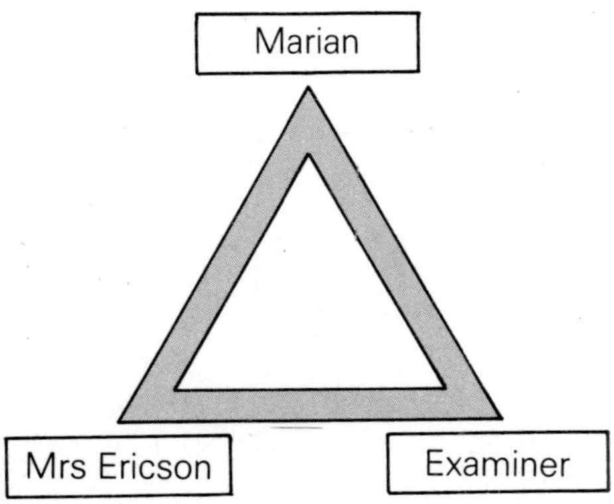

Write a short paragraph on the relationship of Marian and Mrs Ericson.

Write a short paragraph on the examiner's attitude to Mrs Ericson.

Write a more substantial account of the relationship between Marian and the examiner, remembering that a relationship is a two-way affair.

After You, My Dear Alphonse

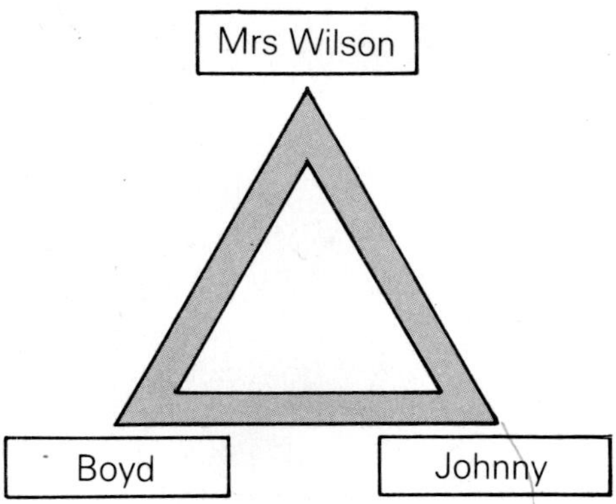

Write a short paragraph on the relationship between Johnny and Boyd.

Write a short paragraph on Mrs Wilson's attitude to Johnny.

Write a more substantial account of the relationship between Mrs Wilson and Boyd, remembering that a relationship is a two-way affair.

6 *In the black corner... In the white corner...*

The Test

The Test can been seen as a contest, with the driving examiner trying to provoke Marian into failing, testing her patience rather than her driving ability. Marian is equally determined to stay cool and pass.

a) How many 'rounds' can you count in this contest?

b) State briefly what each 'round' is, and who wins it.

c) Who wins the contest?

After You, My Dear Alphonse

In a way, this story can also be seen as a contest, with Mrs Wilson trying to fit Boyd and his family into her stereotyped picture, and Boyd (and Johnny) thwarting her at every turn.

a) How many rounds can you count in this contest?

b) Briefly state what each 'round' is.

c) How does Mrs Wilson 'throw in the towel', finally signal defeat?

Talking

How does Mrs Wilson's attitude to blacks differ from the examiner's? Is her attitude any less objectionable?

Telephone Conversation

by Wole Soyinka

The price seemed reasonable, location
Indifferent. The landlady swore she lived
Off premises. Nothing remained
But self-confession. 'Madam,' I warned,
'I hate a wasted journey—I am African.'
Silence. Silenced transmission of
Pressurized good-breeding. Voice, when it came,
Lipstick coated, long gold-rolled
Cigarette-holder pipped. Caught I was, foully.
'HOW DARK?'... I had not misheard... 'ARE YOU LIGHT
OR VERY DARK?' Button B. Button A. Stench
Of rancid breath of public, hide-and-speak.

Red booth. Red pillar box. Red double-tiered
Omnibus squelching tar. It *was* real! Shamed
By ill-mannered silence, surrender
Pushed dumbfoundment to beg simplification.
Considerate she was, varying the emphasis—
'ARE YOU DARK? OR VERY LIGHT?' Revelation came.
'You mean—like plain or milk chocolate?'
Her assent was clinical, crushing in its light
Impersonality. Rapidly, wave-length adjusted,
I chose. 'West African sepia'—and as afterthought,
'Down in my passport.' Silence for spectroscopic
Flight of fancy, till truthfulness clanged her accent
Hard on the mouthpiece. 'WHAT'S THAT?' conceding
'DON'T KNOW WHAT THAT IS.' 'Like brunette.'
'THAT'S DARK, ISN'T IT?' 'Not altogether.
Facially, I am brunette but, madam, you should see
The rest of me. Palm of my hand, soles of my feet
Are a peroxide blond. Friction, caused—
Foolishly, madam—by sitting down, has turned
My bottom raven black—One moment, madam!'—sensing
Her receiver rearing on the thunderclap
About my ears—'Madam,' I pleaded, 'wouldn't you rather
See for yourself?'

Reading

(lines 1–4)

1 What is the speaker looking for in a flat?

2 'Nothing remained but self-confession.'
What does 'confession' tell you about the speaker's attitude to what he is about to say?

(lines 6–11)

3 'Silence.' What do you think is going on in the landlady's mind at this point?

4 'Voice, when it came, lipstick-coated, long gold-rolled cigarette-holder pipped . . .'
What does this suggest about the way the landlady speaks now?
How does this compare with the way she spoke earlier?
Can you account for the change?

5 Why do you think the landlady is so concerned to discover the precise shade of the speaker's skin?

(lines 11–14)

6 What is the speaker's reaction to the landlady's question?

7 Can you suggest why the word 'red' is repeated three times? (Think of a familiar idiom for feeling very angry!)

8 'Red double-tiered omnibus squelching tar.'
Think of the image, the picture, this conjures up, and the colour of tar. Can you relate this line to the speaker and the landlady?

(*lines 14–16*)

9 'Surrender pushed dumbfoundment to beg simplification.'
What do you think the speaker actually *says* at this point?

(*lines 16–21*)

10 'Her assent was clinical, crushing in its light impersonality.'
What do you think the landlady actually *says* at this point?
In your own words, explain *how* she says this, her tone of voice.

(*lines 21–27*)

11 What 'adjustment in wave-length' does the speaker make, in changing from 'plain or milk chocolate' to 'West African sepia'?
12 Why does he add the afterthought, about his passport?
13 'Silence for spectroscopic flight of fancy'.
What is the landlady thinking about this time?
14 What do the words 'clanged' and 'hard' suggest about the landlady's voice now?
Can you account for this latest change?

(*lines 27–35*)

15 This is the most the speaker has actually said so far. What is his tone of voice?
16 What does this suggest about his attitude to:
a) the landlady,
b) his getting the flat?
17 What effect does the speaker's tone have on the landlady?
18 'Madam,' I pleaded, 'wouldn't you rather see for yourself?'
See what for yourself?
Can you find a double meaning here?
Do you think it is intentional?

Writing

Choose *one* of the following topics and write an essay of about three hundred words. You may find the opportunity to use words and ideas, you have picked up during this unit.

1 Argue *for* or *against* the idea that legislation (passing laws) can really help to get rid of prejudice.

2 'It takes 51 Irishmen to write on a wall. One to hold the pen and the other 50 to move the wall.'
Argue *for* or *against* the idea that racial jokes are potentially dangerous and offensive, and should therefore be banned on T.V. and radio.

3 'Racial prejudice is a pigment of the imagination.' Do you agree?

4 Someone wrote on a wall *God is black*. Underneath it, someone had added *Yes, so She is.*
Do you think that in this country there is still strong prejudice against women?

5 Is there any *particular* form of racial or colour or religious prejudice that really offends you personally?

Explain clearly what it is, in what ways it gives particular offence, and what you would like to see done about it.

6 Is the current ideal — that Britain must become a multi-racial, multi-cultural society — in your view, a practical possibility? What suggestions would you offer to assist progress towards that ideal?

Talking

For this project you should work in pairs or small groups.
Choose *four* of the following pairs, discuss the ingredients carefully, and produce an *agreed* stereotype for each character. If you cannot agree, please note the point you can't agree on.

Pair A	Tory M. P./ Labour M. P.
Pair B	teenage football fan/ teenage pop idol
Pair C	university professor/ a judge
Pair D	heavyweight professional boxer/ male ballet dancer
Pair E	Irish labourer/ American tourist
Pair F	middle class suburban housewife/ champion of Women's Lib.
Pair G	woman traffic warden/ matron of a large hospital

If you find no problem in agreeing . . . does this mean you are both prejudiced? If you can't agree on a stereotype, or on some quality in that stereotype, why not? Does one of you actually *know* such a real person?

Reading (Literature)

Choose from your reading in this unit two texts. One must be either of the two short stories, the other must be either *Telephone Conversation* or one of the two speeches by Shylock.

Discuss what each text has to say about the nature of prejudice, and say how each text has contributed to your understanding of prejudice. As well as the ideas in each text, you should consider the writer's skill in presenting them.

Unit 3

Getting in the Way

POVERTY

Each year more than ten million people all over the world die because they do not have enough to eat. Some starve to death, many die from diseases related to malnutrition; all of them die in poverty.

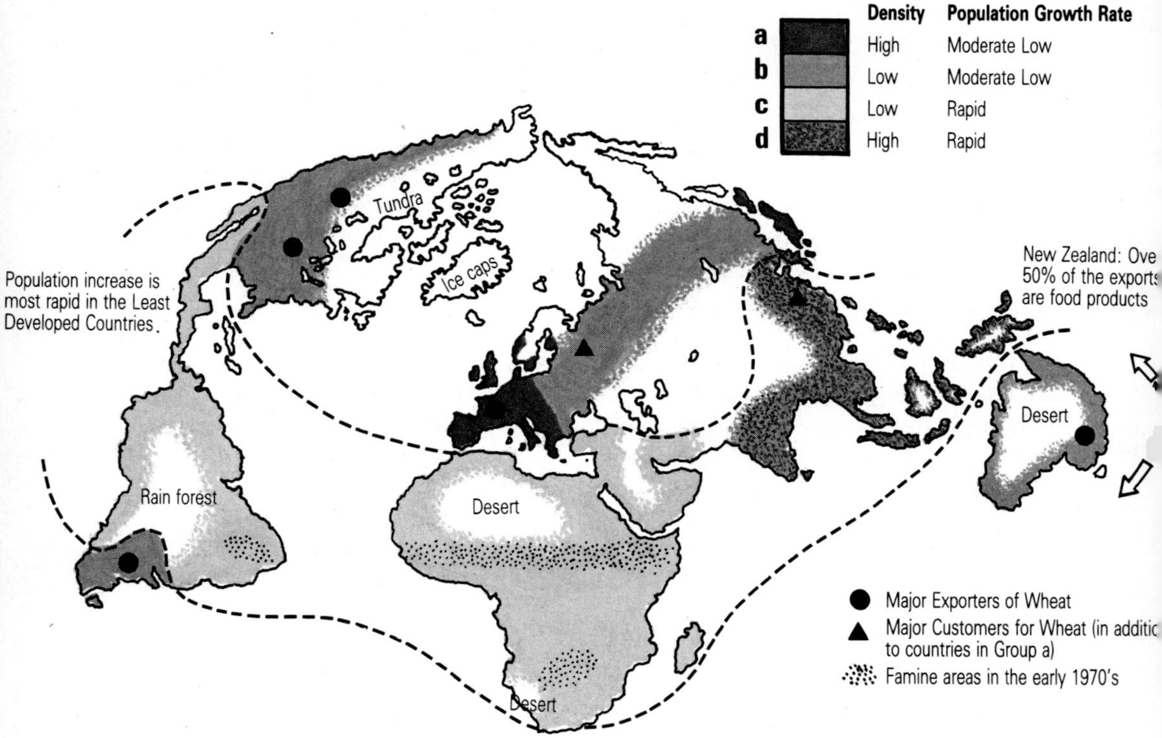

The poor, living mainly in the Third World (Far East, Africa, India, South America) make up seventy per cent of the world's population.

The rich, in Europe, USA and the Communist Bloc, make up thirty per cent of the world's population.

70% of the world's population have roughly 10% of the wealth.

30% of the world's population have roughly 90% of the wealth.

'The greatest of evils and the worst of crimes is poverty.'

(George Bernard Shaw)

I Was A Child Slave

by Keith Waterhouse

As far as I can remember I was bringing home about a quid a week, less deductions. The deductions were for ice cream, sherbet dabs and the instalments on a pair of workman's overalls which I was buying on the never-never.

For those days, and considering that I hadn't reached my twelfth birthday, it was good money. Not as good as all those kids down in Bermondsey were making for labelling bottles until they were stopped from doing it last week, but not bad.

I never moved in bottle-labelling circles, although it was one of my earliest ambitions, for I'd read that Charles Dickens started life pasting labels on jars of boot polish. The nearest I got to the boot polish racket was when I donned my never-never overalls during the school holidays and worked for a cobbler.

I had to clean out the grinding machine, a job which involved getting inside it and crawling along a zinc chute like a horizontal chimney sweep. With half-a-crown clutched in my hot little hand I used to go home looking like a refugee from *The Water Babies.*

But that was only seasonal work. My regular income came from a morning, evening and Sunday newspaper round, and its ancillary perks.

If you lived on my round I could always quote you favourable rates for knocking-up, errand-running or message-carrying. I also had the contract for looking after some rabbits for a strange spinster lady who took the *News Chronicle*.

On Saturday mornings, I stationed myself outside the Co-op with a soap-box on wheels and ferried groceries at a fixed tariff of three-pence per trip. On Saturday afternoons I cycled down to the Walls depot and picked up a supply of ice cream for the local sweet shop.

During the summer evenings I operated a flourishing golf-caddying concession, and during the winter evenings I ran a thriving firewood business. We will not go into the question of where the firewood came from. It fetched sixpence a bucket and for sawn-up chestnut palings which burnt well, that was good value.

In my spare time I collected and sold waste paper, pressed button "B" in all the neighbourhood telephone boxes, and was generally available for any legal or semi-legal enterprise.

The question is, did it do me any harm?

All I can say is that while all work and no play may or may not have made Waterhouse a dull boy, it didn't leave him skint. Which is what I became on the day I left school, when I had to take a proper job and my business empire collapsed.

Talking

1 Do you have a part-time job like baby-sitting or delivering papers or serving in a shop?
Do you think you are fairly paid for the work you do?
Look at the heading of the article — are you a slave?
Was Keith Waterhouse?

2 Do you think that working before or after school would have any effect on your academic progress?

Does Keith Waterhouse think it did him any harm? Or any good?
Do you think anything positive, apart from the extra cash, comes from having a part-time job?

3 Waterhouse was part of a working class family in the north of England. Even at twelve years old he seems to have spent all his spare time working for his pocket money. Was he poor?
If you work to supplement the money your parents give you, does that mean you are poor?
Is this what *poverty* means — always being short of money?

African Beggar

by Raymond Tong

Sprawled in the dust outside the Syrian store.
a target for small children, dogs and flies,
a heap of verminous rags and matted hair,
he watches us with cunning, reptile eyes,
his noiseless, smallpoxed face creased in a sneer.

Sometimes he shows his yellow stumps of teeth
and whines for alms, perceiving that we bear
the curse of pity; a grotesque mask of death,
with hands like claws about his begging bowl

But often he is lying all alone
within the shadow of a crumbling wall,
lost in the trackless jungle of his pain,
clutching the pitiless red earth in vain
and whimpering like a stricken animal.

Reading

1 What point is Tong trying to make by dwelling on the ugliness of the beggar?

2 The poet's description of the beggar seems quite unsympathetic in the first two verses. Tong shows he feels sorry for him only in the last verse. Find evidence in the poem to support this view, concentrating on word choice and imagery.

3 Find the definitions of the following words:
destitute, poor, poverty, subsistence.

Talking

1 Have you ever been approached by a beggar or a vagrant?
Where? What was he/she like? How did you feel?

2 Imagine you are 'down on your luck'. Would you ever beg?

Writing

1 Describe a vagrant you have seen (or the man pictured), trying to bring out your feelings towards him.

2 Write a short story entitled 'The Beggar'.

Assisi

by Norman MacCaig

The dwarf with his hands on backwards
Sat, slumped like a half-filled sack
On tiny twisted legs from which
Sawdust might run,
Outside the three tiers of churches built
In honour of St Francis, brother
Of the poor, talker with birds, over whom
He had the advantage
Of not being dead yet.

A priest explained
How clever it was of Giotto
To make his frescoes tell stories
That would reveal to the illiterate the goodness
Of God and the suffering
Of His Son. I understood
The explanation and
The cleverness.

A rush of tourists, clucking contentedly,
Fluttered after him as he scattered
The grain of the word. It was they who had passed
The ruined temple outside, whose eyes
Wept pus, whose back was higher
Than his head, whose lopsided mouth
Said, *Grazie* in a voice as sweet
As a child's when she speaks to her mother
Or a bird's when it spoke
To St Francis.

Reading

1 St. Francis was the patron saint of .... His church can be found at .... in .... The church is unusual in that it is built on .... levels on a hillside. It is also a famous tourist attraction because of the frescoes of .... Frescoes are .... whose purpose was to illustrate .... stories to the ....

2 Try to find the meanings of the following literary terms and then find an example of each in the poem:
hyperbole, image, irony, ironic contrast.

3 (*Verse 1*)
  a) What image does the poet try to create when he describes the dwarf — 'hands on backwards', 'half-filled sack', 'tiny twisted legs'?
  b) How does this affect our attitude to the dwarf?
  c) Do you think it is important that the dwarf is *outside* the church? Why?

(*Verse 2*)

a) What is the priest doing? What should he be doing?

b) What have the frescoes become? What was their original purpose?

(*Verse 3*)

a) What image of the tourists does MacCaig create? Why?

b) Who/what is the 'ruined temple'? Should we contrast this to the church of Assisi?

c) What is unusual about the dwarf? How does the poet lead us to this revelation?

d) Why does MacCaig end the poem by reminding us of St. Francis?

4 Reread *African Beggar*. Which poem do you prefer? Why? (You may like to consider the contribution made to each poem by the poets' use of imagery, word choice and figurative language.)

We have seen three beggars from different areas of the world. They all relied, almost entirely, on the generosity of others for their survival. Does this mean they all lived in poverty? Did one seem better off than the others? Why?

Marrakech

by George Orwell

As the corpse went past the flies left the restaurant table in a cloud and rushed after it, but they came back a few minutes later.

The little crowd of mourners—all men and boys, no women—threaded their way across the market-place between the piles of pomegranates and the taxis and the camels, wailing a short chant over and over again. What really appeals to the flies is that the corpses here are never put into coffins, they are merely wrapped in a piece of rag and carried on a rough wooden bier on the shoulders of four friends. When the friends get to the burying-ground they hack an oblong hole a foot or two deep, dump the body in it and fling over it a little of the dried-up, lumpy earth, which is like broken brick. No gravestone, no name, no identifying mark of any kind. The burying-ground is merely a huge waste of hummocky earth, like a derelict building-lot. After a month or two no one can even be certain where his own relatives are buried.

When you walk through a town like this—two hundred thousand inhabitants, of whom at least twenty thousand own literally nothing except the rags they stand up in—when you see how the people live, and still more easily they die, it is always difficult to believe that you are walking among human beings. All colonial empires are in reality founded upon that fact. The people all have brown faces—besides, there are so many of them. Are they really the same flesh as yourself? Do they even have names? Or are they merely a kind of undifferentiated brown stuff, about as individual as bees or coral insects? They rise out of the earth, they sweat and starve for a few years, and then they sink back into the nameless mounds of the graveyard and nobody notices that they are gone. And even the graves themselves soon fade back into the soil. Sometimes, out for a walk, as you break your way through the prickly pear, you notice that it is rather bumpy underfoot, and only a certain regularity in the bumps tells you that you are walking over skeletons.

I was feeding one of the gazelles in the public gardens.

Gazelles are almost the only animals that look good to eat when they are still alive; in fact, one can hardly look at their hindquarters without thinking of mint sauce. The gazelle I was feeding seemed to know that this thought was in my mind, for though it took the piece of bread I was holding out it obviously did not like me. It nibbled rapidly at the bread, then lowered its head and tried to butt me, then took another nibble and then butted again. Probably its idea was that if it could drive me away the bread would somehow remain hanging in mid-air.

An Arab navvy working on the path near by lowered his heavy hoe and sidled slowly towards us. He looked from the gazelle to the bread and from the bread to the gazelle, with a sort of quiet amazement, as though he had never seen anything quite like this before. Finally he said shyly in French:

"*I* could eat some of that bread."

I tore off a piece and he stowed it gratefully in some secret place under his rags. This man is an employee of the Municipality.

When you go through the Jewish quarters you gather some idea of what the medieval ghettoes were probably like. Under their Moorish rulers the Jews were only allowed to own land in certain restricted areas, and after centuries of this kind of treatment they have ceased to bother about overcrowding. Many of the streets are a good deal less than six feet wide, the houses are completely windowless, and sore-eyed children cluster everywhere in unbelievable numbers, like clouds of flies. Down the centre of the street there is generally running a little river of urine.

In the bazaar huge families of Jews, all dressed in the long black robe and little black skull-cap, are working in dark fly-infested booths that look like caves. A carpenter sits crosslegged at a prehistoric lathe, turning chair-legs at lightning speed. He works the lathe with a bow in his right hand and guides the chisel with his left foot, and thanks to a lifetime of sitting in this position his left leg is warped out of shape. At his side his grandson, aged six, is already starting on the simpler parts of the job.

I was just passing the coppersmiths' booths when somebody noticed that I was lighting a cigarette. Instantly, from the dark holes all round, there was a frenzied rush of Jews, many of them old grandfathers with flowing grey beards, all clamouring for a cigarette. Even a blind man somewhere at the back of one of the booths heard a rumour of cigarettes and came crawling out, groping in the air with his hand. In about a minute I had used up the whole packet. None of these people, I suppose, works less than twelve hours a day, and every one of them looks on a cigarette as a more or less impossible luxury.

Most of Morocco is so desolate that no wild animal bigger than a hare can live on it. Huge areas which were once covered with forest have turned into a treeless waste where the soil is exactly like broken-up brick. Nevertheless a good deal of it is cultivated, with frightful labour. Everything is done by hand. Long lines of women, bent double like inverted capital L's work their way slowly across the fields, tearing up the prickly weeds with their hands, and the peasant gathering lucerne for fodder pulls it up stalk by stalk instead of reaping it, thus saving an inch or two on each stalk. The plough is a wretched wooden thing, so frail that one can easily carry it on one's shoulder, and fitted underneath with a rough iron spike which stirs the soil to a depth of about four inches. This is as much as the strength of the animals is equal to. It is usual to plough with a cow and a donkey yoked together. Two donkeys would not be quite strong enough, but on the other hand two cows would cost a little more to feed. The peasants possess no harrows, they merely plough the soil several times over in different directions, finally leaving it in rough furrows, after which the whole field has to be shaped with hoes into small oblong patches to conserve water. Except for a day or two after the rare rainstorms there is never enough water. Along the edges of the fields channels are hacked out to a depth of thirty or forty feet to get at the tiny trickles which run through the subsoil.

Every afternoon a file of very old women passes down the road outside my house, each carrying a load of firewood. All of them are mummified with age and the sun, and all of them are tiny. It seems to be generally the case in primitive communities that the women, when they get beyond a certain age, shrink to the size of children. One day a poor old creature who could not have been more than four feet tall crept past me under a vast load of wood. I stopped her and put a five-sou piece (a little more than a farthing) into her hand. She answered with a shrill wail, almost a scream, which was partly gratitude but mainly surprise. I suppose that from her point of view, by taking any notice of her, I seemed almost to be violating a law of nature. She accepted her status as an old woman, that is to say as a beast of burden. When a family is travelling it is quite usual to see a father and a grown-up son riding ahead on donkeys, and an old woman following on foot, carrying the baggage.

But what is strange about these people is their invisibility. For several weeks, always at about the same time of day, the file of old women had hobbled past the house with their firewood, and though they had registered themselves on my eyeballs I cannot truly say that I had seen them. Firewood was passing—that was how I saw it. It was only that one day I happened to be walking behind them, and the curious up-and-down motion of a load of wood drew my attention to the human being beneath it. Then for the first time I noticed the poor old earth-coloured bodies, bodies reduced to bones and leathery skin, bent double under the crushing weight. Yet I suppose I had not been five minutes on Moroccan soil before

I noticed the overloading of the donkeys and was infuriated by it. There is no question that the donkeys are damnably treated. The Moroccan donkey is hardly bigger than a St. Bernard dog, it carries a load which in the British Army would be considered too much for a fifteen-hands mule, and very often its pack-saddle is not taken off its back for weeks together. But what is peculiarly pitiful is that it is the most willing creature on earth, it follows its master like a dog and does not need either bridle or halter. After a dozen years of devoted work it suddenly drops dead, whereupon its master tips it into the ditch and the village dogs have torn its guts out before it is cold.

This kind of thing makes one's blood boil, whereas—on the whole—the plight of the human beings does not. I am not commenting, merely pointing to a fact. People with brown skins are next door to invisible. Anyone can be sorry for the donkey with its galled back, but it is generally owing to some kind of accident if one even notices the old woman under her load of sticks.

Reading

1 An anecdote is a short story or a description of an incident remembered from personal experience. Find two or three anecdotes in *Marrakech* and describe what you think Orwell was trying to achieve by including them.

2 'A good essay should appeal to a man's reason, but should also touch his heart'. How far is this true of *Marrakech*?

Extract from *The Road to Wigan Pier* by George Orwell

The train bore me away, through the monstrous scenery of slag-heaps, chimneys, piled scrap-iron, foul canals, paths of cindery mud criss-crossed by the prints of clogs. This was March, but the weather had been horribly cold and everywhere there were mounds of blackened snow. As we moved slowly through the outskirts of the town we passed row after row of little grey slum houses running at right angles to the embankment. At the back of one of the houses a young woman was kneeling on the stones, poking a stick up the leaden waste-pipe which ran from the sink inside and which I suppose was blocked. I had time to see everything about her—her sacking apron, her clumsy clogs, her arms reddened by the cold. She looked up as the train passed, and I was almost near enough to catch her eye. She had a round pale face, the usual exhausted face of the slum girl who is twenty-five and looks forty, thanks to miscarriages and drudgery; and it wore, for the second in which I saw it, the most desolate, hopeless expression I have ever seen. It struck me then that we are mistaken when we say that 'It isn't the same for them as it would be for us,' and that people bred in the slums can imagine nothing but the slums. For what I saw in her face was not the ignorant suffering of an animal. She knew well enough what was happening to her—understood as well as I did how dreadful a destiny it was to be kneeling there in the bitter cold, on the slimy stones of a slum backyard, poking a stick up a foul drain-pipe.

Reading

1 What effect does Orwell's description of the weather have on the mood of this paragraph?

2 'I had time to see everything about her . . .' Orwell seems to sum up the girl's appearance in this sentence. Why does he choose these three details? (Consider his choice of adjectives.)

3 What effect does the word 'usual' have on the meaning of the sentence beginning, 'She had a round, pale face'?

4 Why does Orwell compare the girl to an 'animal'?

5 'It struck me that we are mistaken' — who are *we*?

6 What, does Orwell think, are the girl's feelings about her life?

7 Why does he find her feelings so disturbing?

8 Reread Orwell's description of the Jewish ghetto in *Marrakech*. Do living conditions in this slum in the north of England seem any better?

Indifference

'The worst sin towards our fellow creatures is not to hate them, but to be indifferent to them; that's the essence of inhumanity.'

(From The *Devil's Disciple* by George Bernard Shaw)

Talking

Discuss the following questions, perhaps in small groups.

1 What is there in the two images which suggests poverty? (See page 48.)

2 What is your reaction to the pictures?

3 Christian Aid used these posters to advertise an appeal for aid for Third World Countries. How successful do you think they would be? Why?

4 Do you agree with Shaw's statement? Why?

Roots, by Arnold Wesker is a play which explores the feelings of deprivation and vague discontent of a poor agricultural family in Norfolk. Beatie Bryant, the main character, comes to a gradual realisation of the importance of education and cultural heritage. She believes that the working-class has been 'sold short'. As her understanding grows, so does her articulacy.

Extract from *Roots*

by Arnold Wesker

BEATIE [*impatiently*]: Roots, roots, roots! Christ, Frankie, you're in the fields all day, you should know about growing things. Roots! The things you come from, the things that feed you. The things that make you proud of yourself-roots!

Listen to me! I'm tellin' you that the world's bin growing for two thousand years and we hevn't noticed it. I'm telling you that we don't know what we are or where we come from. I'm telling you something's cut us off from the beginning. I'm telling you we've got no roots. Blimey Joe! We've all got large allotments, we all grow things around us so we should know about roots. You know how to keep your flowers alive don't you Mother? Jimmy—you know how to keep the roots of your veges strong and healthy. It's not only the corn that need strong roots, you know, it's us too. But what've we got? Go on, tell me, what've we got? We don't know where we push up from and we don't bother neither.

Shall I tell you what Susie said when I went and saw her? She say she don't care if that ole atom bomb drop and she die—that's what she say. And you know why she say it? I'll tell you why, because if she had to care she'd have to do something about it and she find *that* too much effort. Yes she do. She can't be bothered—she's too bored with it all. That's what we all are—we're all too bored.

MRS BRYANT: Blust woman—bored you say, bored? You say Susie's bored, with a radio and television an' that? I go t'hell if she's bored!

BEATIE: Oh yes, we turn on a radio or a TV set maybe, or we go to the pictures—if them's love stories or gangsters—but isn't that the easiest way out? Anything so long as we don't have to make an effort. Well, am I right? You know I'm right.

Education ent only books and music — it's asking questions, all the time. There are millions of us, all over the country, and no one, not one of us, is asking questions, we're all taking the easiest way out. Everyone I ever worked with took the easiest way out. We don't fight for anything, we're so mentally lazy we might as well be dead. Blust, we are dead! And you know what Ronnie say sometimes? He say it serves us right! That's what he say — it's our own bloody fault!

JIMMY: So that's us summed up then — so we know where *we* are then!

MRS BRYANT: Well if he don't reckon we count nor nothin', then it's as well he didn't come. There! It's as well he didn't come.

BEATIE: Oh, *he* thinks we count all right-living in mystic communion with nature. Living in mystic bloody communion with nature (indeed). But us count? Count Mother? I wonder. Do we? Do you think we really count? You don' wanna take any notice of what them ole papers say about the workers bein' all-important these days — that's all squit! 'Cos we aren't. Do you think when the really talented people in the country get to work they get to work for us? Hell if they do! Do you think they don't know we 'ont make the effort? The writers don't write thinkin' we can understand, nor the painters don't paint expecting us to be interested — that they don't, nor don't the composers give out music thinking we can appreciate it. 'Blust,' they say, 'the masses is too stupid for us to come down to them. Blust,' they say, 'if they don't make no effort why should we bother?' So you know who come along? The slop singers and the pop writers and the film makers and women's magazines and the Sunday papers and the picture strip love stories — that's who come along, and you don't have to make no effort for them, it come easy. 'We know where the money lie,' they say, 'hell we do! The workers've got it so let's give them what they want. If they want slop songs and film idols we'll give 'em that then. If they want words of one syllable, we'll give 'em that then. If they want the third-rate, *blust!* We'll give 'em *that* then. Anything's good enough for them 'cos they don't ask for no more!' The whole stinkin' commercial world insults us and we don't care a damn. Well, Ronnie's right — it's our own bloody fault.

Reading

1 What do you think Beatie means by roots? What is needed to 'water' them?

2 Why does this metaphor seem particularly appropriate?

3 Beatie's family are poor, in an economic sense, but she believes they suffer from another sort of poverty. Can you say what this is?

4 How is it their own fault?

5 Ronnie thinks they live 'in mystic communion with nature'. What does this tell us about Ronnie?

6 What do the entertainments enjoyed by 'the masses' all have in common?

7 You have studied various rhetorical devices, techniques like repetition and rhetorical questions. In *Roots* Beatie is trying to persuade her family that they must *do* something to change their situation. How convincing is her speech likely to be a) to her family? b) to the theatre audience?
(In discussing this, pay attention to the rhetorical devices used.)

Talking

1 Does economic poverty lead inevitably to poverty of intellect and imagination?

2 Do you agree with the view illustrated in this extract, that 'art' is not for the masses?

3 Is poverty, then, simply a measurement of economic status?

4 How important is it to have an aim or purpose in life? What happens if your life seems aimless?

Unemployment

by Janet Frame

Each Tuesday at ten o'clock I go to the Employment Exchange,
fill in the form they give me, tell what I have earned
for chopping down the neighbour's tree, feeding his horse,
rescuing a silly sheep from the swamp. Sometimes, with odd jobs,
I make as much as a pound a week, but no one
offers anything permanent. The official (whom I knew at school,
a bear in the back seat) gapes at me: I'm sorry we cannot place you.
And therefore I am not placed, not in this or that. I have
a fine box of tools that I keep well-oiled. I have experience
and knowledge tied in a waiting bundle in the corner of my mind
nearest the door but no one knocks and the door is never opened.

I collect my weekly allowance, I go home,
I cuddle my wife, feed the cat,
and, for no purpose in no place, grow fat.

A

Fair Shares For All

by J. E. Stringfellow

1 Let's share the food, my brother,
Let's share the fruits of the earth,
Steak for me, but rice for you,
Eggs for tea, the devil take you;
It's nice for me, and rice for you;
Fruit and wine, milk.and jam,
Cheese and pickles and fish and ham,
For me;
And a little rice, just a little rice,
(if you're lucky) for you.

2 Let's share the pain, my brother,
You shall have more than your share,
Pains for you, and pills for me;
Germs for you, and jabs for me;
Though you die young, long life for me;
Tranquillisers, deep X-ray
Penicillin, and nothing to pay, For me;
and a little clinic, just a mobile clinic,
(per hundred thousand people) for you.

3 Let's share the war, my brother,
Let's share the horrors of war.
Peace for me, napalm for you;
Trade for me, but raids for you;
"Away" for me, "At home" for you;
Cripples, orphans, refugees,
Villages burned, no leaves on trees,
For you;
And a little pang of conscience, just a little twinge,
(not very often) for me.

4 Let's share our wealth, my brother,
Let's share all that you have.
Gold for me, and beads for you;
Christ for me, and devil take you;
There's two for me, and none for you;
Bingo, bombs, and drugs and booze,
Money to burn, and waste and lose,
For me;
And a little aid, just a little aid,
(when we can spare it) for you.

B The differences between the world's rich and poor are astonishing. People in the Third World are likely to:

1 have less, and often unhealthy, food to eat;
2 suffer from diseases related to malnourishment*;
3 have a shorter life expectancy;
4 obtain inadequate medical care;
5 be illiterate and innumerate;
6 be unemployed for long periods.

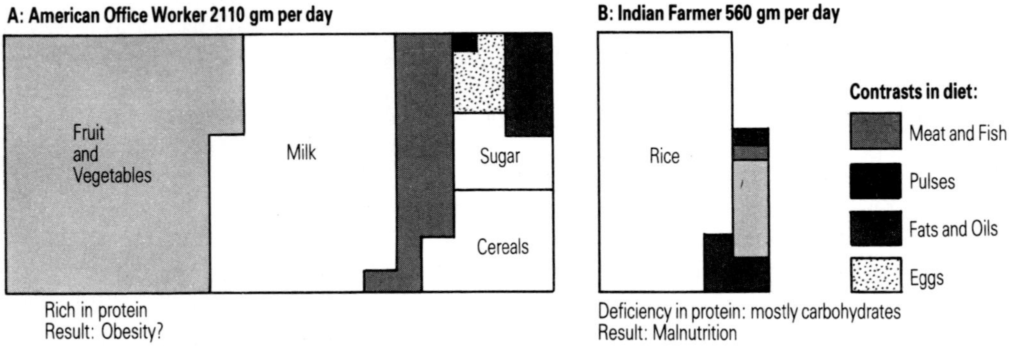

* Malnourishment is different from starvation.
Starvation means lack of food.
Malnourishment is lack of a properly balanced diet. Food may be plentiful — but it is the wrong kinds of food.

C

Extract from *Child with Malaria*
by Clark Mills

In the walled world of darkness and his fever
the chairs were beasts, the lamp shade was a lowered head.
The sheet was an expanse of ice enfolding
the clenched fright and the weakness in the bed.

His malady that night was a deep forest
where danger stood like trees, or soldiers, and low cries
rose from his footsteps, and in all the shadows
presences lurked and stared with round green eyes.

D *AID IS SMALL COMPARED WITH WHAT RICH COUNTRIES SPEND ON OTHER THINGS*

Reading

ITEM A

Fair Shares For All by J. E. Stringfellow

1 Complete the following statements.
   a) The 'I' in the poem is ..... and his 'brother' is ..... .
   b) In verse one, the writer shares out the ....., but this sharing out is far from fair because ..... .
   c) In verse two, the writer shares out the ....., but this sharing out is far from fair because ..... .
   d) In verse three, the writer shares out the ....., but this sharing out is far from fair because ..... .
   e) In verse four, the writer shares out the ....., but this sharing out is far from fair because ..... .
   f) In verses ..... his brother gets less than his fair share.
   g) In verses ..... his brother gets more than his fair share.

2 *Parenthesis* is when a comment is inserted in a sentence which is grammatically complete without it; it is a figure of speech consisting in the use of such insertion. The insertion can be placed between commas, dashes or brackets.
   Quote an example of parenthesis from each verse of the poem, and explain how it affects the meaning of its sentence.

3 Comment on the structure of each verse.
   a) How effective do you find the writer's repeated use of 'Let's share', 'little' and 'just a . . .'?
   b) Note that the first half of each verse is based on contrasting items, which is then followed by a list of things that go to only one of the two — either to 'I' or his 'brother'.
   In what way does verse three differ from the other verses?
   What does this change reflect?

4 'Away'/'At home' . . .
   Such expressions are usually used about what?
   What, perhaps, does the writer imply by using them here?

5 Comment on the effectiveness of the contrasts:
   a) germs/jabs, (*verse 2*),
   b) trade/raid (*verse 3*),
   c) Christ/devil take you (*verse 4*).

ITEM B

1 Give an example of a 'disease related to malnourishment'.
2 What is meant by 'a shorter life expectancy'?
   What is normally taken as 'life expectancy' in Western countries?
3 Explain 'illiterate' and 'innumerate'.

ITEM C

Extract from *Child with Malaria* by Clark Mills
Write a description, based on the poem, of the experience of this child suffering

from malaria, but without using the writer's metaphors. You may use your own, if you wish.

ITEM D

Diagram

Write a short paragraph, interpreting the two diagrams, and commenting on aid to the Third World.

Writing

Make a storyboard, using newspaper cuttings, pictures and drawings on the theme of poverty. Supply your own commentary.

Talking

1 Is human nature such that poverty is inevitable?

2 Can an ideal world exist while there is poverty?

3 What can we do to end poverty:
   a) in this country?
   b) in the Third World?

Writing

Write a discursive essay in which you try to answer one of these questions.

1 Why do houses, or housing estates become slums?

2 Do you agree with the statement 'people bred in slums can imagine nothing but the slums'? Outline reasons for your answer.

3 When slums are demolished, the people living there are sometimes rehoused in tower blocks.
   a) Do you think they are an improvement on the slums?
   b) What are the advantages/disadvantages of living in one?

4 Can the environment in which people live influence the way they think or behave?

Note: Remember you should try to maintain a balanced approach, considering both sides of any argument, before you arrive at your conclusion.

Unit 4

Getting in the Way

CLASS

Sandra Harris, *Today* interviewer:
'Tell me, Miss Cartland, have class barriers broken down?'

Miss Barbara Cartland: 'Of course they have, or I wouldn't be sitting here talking to someone like you.'

(From *Class* by Jilly Cooper, 1980)

The Working Class

Look at the cartoon above. The characters portrayed may be described as an archetypal working-class couple. What in their appearance suggests they are working-class? How true a representation of the working-class is this cartoon? Look up the meaning of *caricature*.

Extract from *The Road to Wigan Pier* by George Orwell

'Here you come to the real secret of class distinctions in the West — the reason why a European of bourgeois upbringing, even when he calls himself a Communist, cannot without a hard effort think of a working man as his equal. It is summed up in four frightful words which people nowadays are chary of uttering, but which were bandied about quite freely in my childhood. The words were: *the lower classes smell.*

That was what we were taught—*the lower classes smell.* And here, obviously, you are at an impassable barrier. For no feeling of like or dislike is quite so fundamental as a *physical* feeling. Race-hatred, religious hatred, differences of education, of temperament, of intellect, even differences of moral code, can be got over; but physical repulsion cannot.'

Reading

1 Why do you think people are now 'chary' of uttering these words?

2 What does the expression 'bandied about' mean?

3 Do you find anything odd about the expression 'a physical feeling'? What does Orwell mean here?

4 What in Orwell's view is the difference between this type of prejudice and prejudices based on race or religious hatred?

5 Why, then, do these four simple words form an impassable barrier?

6 Explain what Orwell means by 'the West', 'bourgeois upbringing', and why he writes *'even when he* calls himself a Communist'.

Talking

Do you agree that 'the working classes smell'?
How could this idea have gained credibility?

The Other John Peel

by Alan Sillitoe

When the world was asleep one Sunday morning Bob slid away from the warm aura of his wife and padded downstairs—boots in hand—to fix up a flask and some bacon sandwiches.

Electric light gave the living-room an ageless air, only different from last night in that it was empty—of people. He looked around at the house full of furniture: television set, washing machine glinting white from the scullery, even a car on the street—the lot, and it belonged to him. Eric and Freda also slept, and he'd promised to take them up the Trent and hire a rowing-boat this afternoon if they were good. Wearing his second-best suit, knapsack all set, he remembered Freda's plea a few days ago: 'Will you bring me one o' them tails, our dad?' He had to laugh, the fawce little bogger, as he combed his dark wavy hair at the mirror and put on his glasses. I must tell her not to blab it to her pals though.

He opened the cellar door for his guns and pouches, put them under his arm to keep them low—having a licence for the twelve-bore, but not the ·303 service rifle—and went out into the backyard. The world was a cemetery on short lease to the night, dead quiet except for the whine of factory generators: a row of upstairs windows were closed tight to hold in the breath of sleep. A pale grey saloon stood by the kerb, the best of several left out on the cobbles, and Bob stowed his guns well down behind the back seat before lighting a cigarette.

The streets were yours at six on a Sunday morning, flying through the cradle of a deadbeat world with nothing to stop you getting what fun and excitement you wanted. The one drawback to the ·303 was that out of fifty bullets from the army he'd but twenty left, though if he rationed himself to a shot every Sunday there'd still be six months' sport for the taking. And you never knew: maybe he could tap his cousin in the terriers for a belt of souvenirs.

He bounded through the traffic lights, between church and pub, climbing the smooth tarmac up Mansfield Road, then pouring his headlights into the dip and heading north under a sky of stars. Houses fell endlessly back on either side, a gauntlet trying to cup him but getting nowhere. The wireless had forecast a fine day and looked like being right for a change, which was the least they could do for you. It was good to get out after a week cooped-up, to be a long-range hunter in a car that blended with the lanes. He was doing well for himself: wife and kids, a good toolsetting job, and a four-roomed house at fifteen bob a week. Fine. And most Sunday mornings he ranged from Yorkshire to Lincolnshire, and Staffordshire to Leicestershire, every map-point a sitting duck for his coolly sighted guns.

On the dot of six-thirty he saw Ernie by the Valley Road picture house. 'Hey up,' Ernie said as he pulled in. 'That was well timed.' Almost a foot taller than Bob, he loomed over the car dressed in an old mac.

'It's going to be fine,' Bob said, 'according to the radio.'

Ernie let himself in. 'The wireless's allus wrong. Spouts nowt but lies. I got welloes on in case it rains.'

They scooted up the dual carriageway. 'Is this the best you can do?' Ernie asked. 'You can fetch ninety out of this, I'm sure. 'Ark at that engine: purring like a she-cat on the batter.'

'Take your sweat,' Bob said. 'This is a mystery trip.'

Ernie agreed. 'I'm glad there's no racing on a Sunday. It's good to get out a bit like this.'

'It is, an' all. Missis well?'

'Not too bad. Says she feels like a battleship with such a big belly'—and went silent. Bob knew him well enough: he'd never talk just to be friendly; they could drive for an hour and he'd stay shut, often in an icy far-off mood that didn't give him anything to say or think of. They worked a dozen feet from each other all week, Bob on his precision jobs, Ernie watching a row of crankshift millers. 'What guns you got then?' he asked.

Bob peered ahead, a calm and measured glance along the lit-up wastes of the road to Ollerton. 'A twelve-bore and a ·303.'

'I wish you had,' Ernie laughed. 'You never know when you're going to need a ·303 these days. Best gun out.'

'Keep your trap shut about it though,' Bob said. 'I got it in the army. I wouldn't tell you except that I know I can trust you by now.'

Maybe he wasn't joking, Ernie thought. Bob was clever with hands and brain, the stop-gap of the shop with micro-meter and centre-lathe, a toolmaker who could turn off a candlestick or fag-lighter as soon as look at you. 'Do you mean it about a ·303?'

Bob pulled into a lay-by and got out. 'Keep clear of the headlights,' he said, 'but catch this.' Ernie caught it, pushed forward the safety catch, the magazine resting in the net of his fingers. 'God Almighty! Anything up the spout?'

'I've a clip in my pocket. Strictly for rabbits'—Bob smiled, taking it back.

'A waste,' Ernie said. 'The twelve-bore would do. Mixer-matosis has killed 'em all off, anyway.'

They drove on. 'Had it since I left the army,' Bob told him. 'The stores was in a chronic state in Germany at the end of the war. Found myself with two, so kept one. I have a pot-shot with it now and again. I enjoy hunting—for a bit o' recreation.'

Ernie laughed, wildly and uncontrolled, jerking excited shouts into the air as if trying to throw something out of his mouth, holding his stomach to stop himself doubling up, wearing down the shock of what a free-lance ·303 meant. He put his arm around Bob's shoulder by way of congratulation: 'You'd better not let many people know about it, or the coppers'll get on to you.'

'Don't worry. If ever they search, it's a souvenir. I'd get rid of the bolt, and turn another off on the lathe when I needed it.'

'Marvellous,' Ernie said. 'A ·303! Just the thing to have in case of a revolution. I hope I can get my hands on one when the trouble starts.'

Bob was sardonic: 'You and your revolution! There wain't be one in our lifetimes, I can tell you that.' Ernie had talked revolution to him for months, had argued with fiery puritanical force, guiding Bob's opinion from voting Labour to a head-nodding acceptance of rough and ready Communism. 'I can't see why you think there'll be a revolution though.'

'I've told you though,' Ernie said loudly. 'There's got to be something. I feel it. We wok in a factory, don't we? Well, we're the backbone of the country, but you see, Bob, there's too many people on our backs. And it's about time they was slung off. The last strike we had a bloke in a pub said to me: "Why are you fellows allus on strike?" And I said to 'im: "What sort o' wok do you do?" And he said: "I'm a travelling salesman." So I said, ready to smash 'im: "Well, the reason I come out on strike is because I want to get bastards like yo' off my back." That shut 'im up. He just crawled back into his sherry.'

At dawn they stopped the car in a ladle of land between Tuxford and the Dukeries, pulling on to a grass verge by a gate. A tall hawthorn hedge covered in

green shoots bordered the lane, and the bosom of the meadow within rose steeply to a dark skyline, heavy rolls of cloud across it. Ernie stood by the gate: 'The clouds smell fresh'—pulling his mac collar up. 'Think we'll get owt 'ere?'

'It's good hunting country,' Bob told him. 'I know for a fact.'

They opened flasks and tore hungrily into sandwiches. 'Here, have a swig of this,' Ernie said, pouring some into his own cup. 'It'll do you good.'

Bob held it to the light. 'What is it?'

'Turps and dash. Here's the skin off your lips.'

'Don't talk so loud. You'll chase all the wild life away. Not a bad drop, is it?'

'A rabbit wouldn't get far with a ·303 at its arse.' A sort of loving excitement paralysed his fingers when he picked up the rifle: 'Can you get me one?'

'They don't grow on trees, Ernie.'

'I'd like one, though. For the next war. I'd just wait for somebody to try and call me up!' They leaned on the gate, smoking. 'Christ, when the Russians come I'll be liberated.'

'It's a good job everybody ain't like you,' Bob said with a smile. 'You're a rare 'un, yo' are.'

Ernie saw a movement across the field, beginning from the right and parting a diagonal line of grass, ascending towards the crest on their left. The light from behind showed it up clear and neat. 'See it?' he hissed, ramming a shell in the twelve-bore. Bob said nothing, noiselessly lifted the ·303. No need to use that, Ernie thought. It'd bring a man down a mile off; a twelve-bore's good enough for a skinful of mixer-matosis.

A sudden wind blew against the dawn, ruffling the line of their prey. Bob's eye was still on it: a single round went into the breech. 'I'll take it,' he said softly. It was already out of buck-shot from Ernie's twelve-bore. Both lost it, but said nothing. A lull in the wind didn't show it up. 'I expect it's a hare.'

Bob lowered his ·303, but Ernie signalled him to be quiet: it seemed as if a match were lit in the middle of the field, a slow-burning brown flame moving cautiously through shallow grass, more erratic now, but still edging towards the crest. The cold, star-flecked sky needed only a slow half turn to bring full daylight. What the bloody hell is it? Ernie wondered. Fields and lane were dead quiet: they were kings of the countryside: no houses, no one in sight. He strained his eyes hoping to discover what it was. A squirrel? Some gingernut, anyway.

A smile came on to Bob's face, as when occasionally at work his patience paid off over some exacting job, a flange going into place with not half a thou' to spare. Now it was more heightened than that: a triumph of hunting. Two sharp ears were seen on the skyline, a hang-dog tail, a vulpine mouth breakfasting on wind—with Ernie's heart a bongo drum playing rhythms on his chest wall: A fox.

The air split open, and from all directions came a tidal wave of noise, rushing in on every ear but that to which the bullet had been aimed. Together they were over the gate, and speeding up the slope as if in a dawn attack. Gasping, Bob knelt and turned the dead fox over: as precise a job as he had ever done. 'I always get 'em in the head if I can. I promised one of the tails to a neighbour.'

'Ain't this the first fox you've shot, then?' Ernie couldn't fathom his quiet talk: a fox stone-dead from a ·303 happened once in a lifetime. They walked down the hill. 'I've had about half a dozen,' he said by the car door, dragging a large polythene bag from under the seat and stuffing the dead fox into it. 'From round here most of 'em. I'll knock off a bit and go to Lincolnshire next time.' The fox lay as if under a glass case, head bashed and tail without colour. 'It never stood a chance with a ·303,' Ernie grinned.

He took the wheel going back, flying down lanes to the main road, setting its nose at Mansfield as if intent on cutting Nottinghamshire in two. Bob lounged behind using a pull-through on the ·303. 'I've allus liked hunting,' he shouted to Ernie. 'My old man used to go poaching before the war, so we could have summat to eat. He once did a month in quod, the poor bastard. Never got a chance to enjoy real hunting, like me.'

'I want the next tail, for the kid that's coming,' Ernie said, laughing.

Bob was pleased with himself: 'You talk about revolution: the nobs around here would go daft if they knew I was knocking their sport off.'

It was broad daylight: 'Have another turps and dash,' Ernie said, 'you clever bleeder. You'll find the bottle in my haversack.'

The road opened along a high flat ridge through a colliery village, whose grey houses still had no smoke at their chimneys. Silent headstocks to the left towered above the fenced-off coppices of Sherwood Forest.

Reading

1 Look at the title of the story. Who was the original John Peel? (Think of the song! Who, then, is 'the other'?)

2 Bob and the original John Peel use different hunting methods? What are they?

3 Is their enjoyment of hunting derived from different sources? Explain fully.

4 Bob's father, who also 'hunted' is nevertheless different from the other two. Why?

5 How does Bob regard his ·303 rifle? Has his job in the factory anything to do with this?

6 How does Ernie regard the rifle?

7 Explain clearly the different attitudes of Bob and Ernie to the idea of a revolution.

8 Which comes closer to being part of a revolution, Bob or Ernie? Give reasons for your answer.

9 What is Bob's attitude to the landowners whose land he hunts, and to the bosses 'at wok'? How is this different from Ernie's attitude?

10 Bob and Ernie are both working-class men, they work in the same factory. Yet this story is concerned first and foremost to show how different they are. Can you think why?

11 They pass Sherwood Forest on their way home. Who does Sherwood Forest remind you of? How is Bob different?

12 'The plot of *The Other John Peel* is, at a first reading, very simple. Show how this apparent simplicity conceals a much more complex meaning.'
In writing a full discussion of this quotation, you might like to consider such things as theme, structure, the author's use of symbol and imagery etc.

The Lower Middle Class

Extract from *Class*
by Jilly Cooper

Bryan and Jen Teale: the lower middles

The Teales are probably the most pushy, the most frugal, and most respectable of all the classes, because they are so anxious to escape from the working class. The successful ones iron out their accents and become middle like Mr Heath and Mrs Thatcher, the rest stay put, as bank and insurance clerks, door-to-door salesmen, toast-masters, lower management, police sergeants and sergeant majors. In the old days, the lower middles rose with the small business or the little shop, but the rise in rates, social security benefits and postage has scuppered all that.

The lower middles never had any servants, but as they are obsessed with cleanliness, and like everything nice, they buy a small modern house, and fill it with modern units which are easy to keep clean. Jen and Bryan have two children, WAYNE and CHRISTINE, and a very clean car.

As Jen and Bryan didn't go to boarding school, didn't make friends outside the district, and don't mix with the street, they have very few friends, keeping themselves to themselves. They tend to be very inner-directed, doing everything together, decorating the house, furnishing the car, and coaching and playing football with the children. Jen reads knitting patterns, *Woman's Own*, and *Reader's Digest* condensed books. To avoid any working-class stigma, she puts up defensive barriers: privet hedges, net curtains, talks in a 'refained' accent, raises her little finger when she drinks and runs with her hands turned out, as though she were drying her nail polish. Her aim is to be dainty, and wear six pairs of knickers. She admires Mary Whitehouse enormously, disapproves of long hair and puts money in the Woolwich every week. She sees herself as the 'Woolwich girl'. The children are always being pulled up for some real or imagined coarseness of speech. The Teales don't entertain much, only Bryan's colleagues who might be useful, and occasionally Bryan's boss.

Reading

1 What do you think the writer is trying to suggest by the following items in her description:
   a) the names of the four members of the Teale family,
   b) the words 'pushy', 'frugal' and 'respectable',
   c) the expression 'very inner-directed',
   d) Jen Teale's reading material,
   e) 'Bryan's colleagues *who might be useful*',
   f) 'Her aim is to be dainty and wear six pairs of knickers',
   g) 'and a very clean car',
   h) a 'refained' accent,
   i) 'She admires Mary Whitehouse enormously',
   j) 'She sees herself as the *Woolwich girl*'.

2 The writer uses several rather colloquial expressions, the sort of expressions we use in familiar talk—'pushy', 'scuppered,' 'don't', 'like everything nice'. What effect does this have?

3 What would you say is the writer's *attitude* to the Teales? Does she loathe them? Pity them? Find them amusing? Is she trying to be funny? Sarcastic? Is she holding them up for ridicule?
   In your answer, try to be as precise as you can, and support what you think by referring to the passage.

My Parents Kept me

by Stephen Spender

My parents kept me from children who were rough
Who threw words like stones and who wore torn clothes.
Their thighs showed through rags. They ran in the street
And climbed cliffs and stripped by the country streams.

I feared more than tigers their muscles like iron
Their jerking hands and their knees tight on my arms.
I feared the salt coarse pointing of those boys
Who copied my lisp behind me on the road.

They were lithe, they sprang out behind hedges
Like dogs to bark at my world. They threw mud
While I looked the other way, pretending to smile.
I longed to forgive them, but they never smiled.

1 Look at the simile — 'threw words like stones'.
Does this remind you of a proverb?
What point is the writer trying to make by using this simile?

2 Look at the simile — 'muscles like iron'.
What point is the writer making here?
Do you think that this simile is as good as the last one?

3 Look at the simile — 'They sprang out behind hedges like dogs to bark at my world'.
What is Spender trying to convey about the boys?
Does this image, the picture it suggests, also hint at *why* the boys pick on him?

4 Define a simile.

5 How did the boys get 'their knees tight on my arms'?

6 Explain what the poet means by the expression 'salt coarse pointing'.

7 Write a paragraph discussing how the writer's choice of word and detail has helped you to form a clear impression of:
a) how these other boys *looked*,
b) how this boy, the 'I', *felt*.

Talking

How well do you think this boy would have fitted into the Teale family? Would they have accepted him as one of their own class? Would he have been happy there, do you think?

The (Upper) Middle Class

Talking

It is evident that the artist who drew this cartoon felt that members of a particular class could be easily identified by their appearance.

What is there in the appearance of this couple which makes them, for the cartoonist, typically middle class?

Do you think it is true that you can tell what class a person is from their appearance?

How Beastly the Bourgeois Is

by D. H. Lawrence

1 How beastly the bourgeois is
especially the male of the species —

2 Presentable, eminently presentable —
shall I make you a present of him?

3 Isn't he handsome? Isn't he healthy? Isn't he a fine specimen?
Doesn't he look the fresh clean Englishman, outside?
Isn't it God's own image? Tramping his thirty miles a day
after partridges, or a little rubber ball?
Wouldn't you like to be like that, well off, and quite the thing?

4 Oh, but wait!
Let him meet a new emotion, let him be faced with another man's
  need,
let him come home to a bit of moral difficulty, let life face him with a
  new demand on his understanding
and then watch him go soggy, like a wet meringue.
Watch him turn into a mess, either a fool or a bully.
Just watch the display of him, confronted with a new demand on his
  intelligence,
a new life-demand.

5 How beastly the bourgeois is
especially the male of the species —

Nicely groomed, like a mushroom
standing there so sleek and erect and eyeable —
and like a fungus, living on the remains of bygone life
sucking his life out of the dead leaves of greater life than his own.

6 And even so, he's stale, he's been there too long.
Touch him, and you'll find he's all gone inside
just like an old mushroom, all wormy inside, and hollow
under a smooth skin and an upright appearance.

7 Full of seething, wormy, hollow feelings
rather nasty —
How beastly the bourgeois is!

Standing in their thousands, these appearances, in damp England
what a pity they can't all be kicked over
like sickening toadstools, and left to melt back, swiftly
into the soil of England.

Reading

1. Find out the meaning of *bourgeois*.
2. Why do you think Lawrence particularly chose to use the word 'beastly' in the title?
3. What is the effect on the reader of Lawrence adding 'outside' at the end of line 6?
4. Can you suggest a reason why there is no capital E at englishman or capital G at god?
5. What is Lawrence trying to achieve by changing the person in 'Isn't *it* god's own image'?
6. What is the effect of piling up these questions in the third stanza?
7. Lawrence is ostensibly presenting the positive aspects of the bourgeois in this stanza, but is really attacking them even here. Find evidence to support this view.
8. Why, do you think, is the first line in stanza four so short?
9. What figure of speech is 'watch him go soggy, like a wet meringue'?
10. Stanza three suggests that the bourgeois male appears quite attractive, but stanza four suggests he is really a 'fool or a bully'. In what circumstances, according to Lawrence, does the bourgeois male show his true colours?
11. Stanza five contains an 'extended simile' where the original comparison is elaborated to develop the idea contained in the image. This simile compares the bourgeois male to a mushroom. What are the similarities outlined in this stanza?
12. Stanzas 6 and 7 develop this idea. In your own words try to explain how the idea is developed.
13. By the last stanza the mushrooms have become 'sickening toadstools'. Can you suggest a reason for this?
14. The tone or mood of a piece of writing is often important as it can provide the reader with a clearer idea of the purpose of the writer.
    What is the tone of this poem? Give reasons for your answer.
15. What social class do you think Lawrence belonged to? Why?

"Nouveau Riche"

Climbing the Social Ladder

Talking

Nobody seems to like the 'nouveau riche' very much — can you suggest reasons why this is the case? Would you like to get on, become rich, climb the social ladder, even if nobody loved you?

Writing

Look carefully at the rather unflattering caricatures above. Try to describe *either* the man *or* the woman. *Look for the good details to use.*

Extract from *Room at the Top* by John Braine

'Good evening, Susan,' I said.

'Hello, Joe.' She hesitated perceptibly. 'Have you met my mother and father?'

'How do you do, Mr Lampton.' There was real warmth in Mrs Brown's voice. Seen at close quarters she looked even more formidable; she had a face which I felt could set like stone with the pride of caste.

'Ah've met you at t'Town Hall, lad,' Brown said. He gave me a quick appraising look from brown eyes the colour of Susan's. He looked as sure of himself as Jack, but in a different way; the Yorkshire accent, which I suspected him of overdoing a bit, was one of the marks of that self-assurance. 'Well, what are you drinking?'

'Scotch, please.'

He snapped his fingers and a waiter came up apparently out of thin air. I glanced at Hoylake. There was for a second a sort of dry glow on his face. He made his excuses and moved off quickly; the room was crowded but he made his way through it without brushing anyone. He wasn't looking where he was going either; I remembered the old story of Queen Victoria, who always sat down immediately she felt the desire to, never for an instant bothering whether or not a chair might be there. The light winked on his black spectacles and bald head, his evening suit was the uniform of some complicated and cruel Byzantine hierarchy; the King and Queen were looking at me thoughtfully and coolly now, the servant was handing me a glass of hot amber, which the thought of drinking made my stomach twist away from in fear as if it were some potion which would force me to divulge the whole unforgivable truth, the Princess was whispering something polite and giving me a social smile as if we'd only that moment met, and the Prince from his superior height was preparing to say something gracious to the poor vulgar ex-sergeant who might perhaps be ill at ease among his betters.

'By the way, weren't you at Frinton Bassett?' he asked.

'The Fifty-first,' I said.

'A *very* great friend of mine was with that squadron. Darrow, Chick Darrow. Thoroughly decent chap, went to school with him. Went for a Burton over the Ruhr.'

We noncoms used to say *got the chopper.* Going for a Burton was journalist's talk. It sickened me a bit; though I suppose that he was merely making an attempt to talk what he thought was my language. 'I don't remember him.'

'Oh, you must have met him. You couldn't miss old Chick. Bright red hair and a terrific baritone. Could've been professional.'

'I never met him,' I said, and kept saying for the next fifteen minutes during which he, assisted from time to time by Brown and his wife, played the Do You Know So-and-so game hard and fast from all angles, social, political, and even religious—they were *astounded* that I didn't know Canon Jones at Leddersford, he was very High of course but he was the only clergyman of any intellectual distinction whatever in the North of England . . . It's a well-known game, its object being the humiliation of those with less money than yourself; I wouldn't exactly say that they were successful in this, but I certainly paid dearly for Brown's whisky and the whisky which Jack also bought me. The extra refinement, the gracenote, was Jack's waving away of my offer to buy the drinks. ('No, no old boy, frightfully dear stuff this.')

I've never in all my life felt so completely friendless; I was at bay among the glasses of sherry and whisky, with the vicious little darts laden with the pride-paralysing curare of Do you Know—? and Surely you've met—? and You must have come across—? thrown at me unceasingly. Susan said very little but I could see that she knew what was going on. She would have helped me if she could, but didn't possess the necessary experience or strength of character to do so.

I'd had two pints of old at the St Clair before I went into the dance; combined with four whiskies and my increasing irritation they made me forget my usual caution. I wasn't drunk; but I wasn't fully in control of myself. Jack asked me if I knew the Smiling Zombie's son.

'Amazing chap,' he said. 'Mind you, he'll kill himself in that old Alfa. Drives like a maniac. You must know him, he's always around Dufton.'

'I don't know any tallymen,' I said.

There was a silence.

'I don't follow you, old man.'

'A tallyman sells clothes on credit,' I said. 'In effect it's money-lending. You buy direct from the manufacturer and sell at a retail price about fifty per cent above what I, or any other person with eyes in his head, would pay. Then you charge interest—'

'It's business,' Jack cut in. 'You wouldn't refuse the profits, would you?'

'It's a dirty business,' I said.

Mrs Brown's face had up to then been quite blank. It was a well-shaped face with large eyes and a pale clear skin which accentuated the soft blackness of her hair. As I spoke she admitted an expression of faint disgust to her face; she wasn't, the expression said, a friend of this vulgar person with the bulging shirt-front and the chromium cuff-links, nor did she wish to be after being a witness of the crude and ill-balanced way in which he had answered a perfectly civil remark of dear Jack's; Jack had been remarkably kind, speaking to him almost as if he were a human being, and naturally it had gone to the creature's head. She took Brown's arm.

'This is our dance, dear. Good-bye for the present, Mr Lampton.'

Brown grinned at me. 'Don't worry about the way the world's run, lad. Enjoy yourself when you're young.' He gave me a pat on the shoulder and moved off into the crowd. He had the same way of talking and the same Edwardian solidity as my father; I found myself wishing that I wasn't, for the sake of my self-esteem, compelled to hate him.

Reading

1 To which social class do the Browns belong? And Joe?

2 What is meant by 'Pride of Caste'?

3 Why does Brown overdo his Yorkshire accent?

4 The Browns are likened to 'The King and Queen'. What does this tell you about them?

5 Why is the whisky described as 'a glass of hot amber'?

6 The Princess (Susan) gives Joe a 'social smile'.
What is the difference between a 'social' smile and an ordinary smile? Why is this significant?

7 How could the Browns and Jack be described as Joe's 'betters'?

8 Why should the phrase 'going for a Burton' sicken Joe?

9 How do the other guests humiliate Joe? Is this deliberate?

10 Jack also belittles Joe — how?

11 'I was at bay among the glasses of sherry and whisky! Why sherry and whisky?

12 Joe finally shocks the other guests — how?

13 What is so despicable about the way the Smiling Zombie's son earns his living?

14 Who wins this confrontation? Give reasons.

15 Why does Joe hate Mr Brown, and why does he feel sorry about this?

Reading (Literature)

Basing your answer on the information given in this extract, write on the *character* of *either* Mr Brown *or* Jack Wales.

Joe Lampton, in the last passage, is self-conscious when he enters the room but his discomfort increases as he becomes aware of the differences in speech between the classes. These are mainly differences in accent but also in sentence structure and vocabulary as 'going for a Burton' indicates.

In *Pygmalion*, by George Bernard Shaw, Professor Higgins wagers he can take a cockney flower seller (Eliza), and pass her off as a Duchess by altering the way she speaks. He smoothes her heavy accent, alters the way she structures sentences, teaches her etiquette — and eventually succeeds in fooling society.

At this point in the play, Eliza has been taught a middle-class accent but this merely highlights the differences in structure and vocabulary. Whereas Joe is acutely aware of his 'inferior' position, Eliza seems blissfully unaware of the incongruities of her speech. Therein lies the humour.

Extract from *Pygmalion* by George Bernard Shaw

MRS HIGGINS [*at last, conversationally*] Will it rain, do you think?

LIZA The shallow depression in the west of these islands is likely to move slowly in an easterly direction. There are no indications of any great change in the barometrical situation.

FREDDY Ha! ha! how awfully funny!

LIZA What is wrong with that, young man? I bet I got it right.

FREDDY Killing!

MRS EYNSFORD HILL I'm sure I hope it won't turn cold. There's so much influenza about. It runs right through our whole family regularly every spring.

LIZA [*darkly*] My aunt died of influenza: so they said.

MRS EYNSFORD HILL [*clicks her tongue sympathetically*]!!!

LIZA [*in the same tragic tone*] But it's my belief they done the old woman in.

MRS HIGGINS [*puzzled*] Done her in?

LIZA Y-e-e-e-es, Lord love you! Why should she die of influenza? She come through diphtheria right enough the year before. I saw her with my own eyes. Fairly blue with it, she was. They all thought she was dead; but my father he kept ladling gin down her throat till she came to so sudden that she bit the bowl off the spoon.

MRS EYNSFORD HILL [*startled*] Dear me!

LIZA [*piling up the indictment*] What call would a woman with that strength in her have to die of influenza? What become of her new straw hat that should have come to me? Somebody pinched it; and what I say is, them as pinched it done her in.

MRS EYNSFORD HILL What does doing her in mean?

HIGGINS [*hastily*] Oh, that's the new small talk. To do a person in means to kill them.

MRS EYNSFORD HILL [*to Eliza, horrified*] You surely don't believe that your aunt was killed?

LIZA Do I not! Them she lived with would have killed her for a hat-pin, let alone a hat.

MRS EYNSFORD HILL But it can't have been right for your father to pour spirits down her throat like that. It might have killed her.

LIZA Not her. Gin was mother's milk to her. Besides, he'd poured so much down his own throat that he knew the good of it.

MRS EYNSFORD HILL Do you mean that he drank?

LIZA Drank! My word! Something chronic.

MRS EYNSFORD HILL How dreadful for you!

LIZA Not a bit. It never did him no harm what I could see. But then he did not keep it up regular. [*Cheerfully*] On the burst, as you might say, from time to time. And always more agreeable when he had a drop in. When he was out of work, my mother used to give him fourpence and tell him to go out and not come back until he'd drunk himself cheerful and loving-like. There's lots of women has to make their husbands drunk to make them fit to live with. [*Now quite at her ease*] You see, it's like this. If a man has a bit of a conscience, it always takes him when he's sober; and then it makes him low-spirited. A drop of booze just takes that off and makes him happy. [*To Freddy, who is in convulsions of suppressed laughter*] Here! What are you sniggering at!

FREDDY The new small talk. You do it so awfully well.

LIZA If I was doing it proper, what was you laughing at? [*To Higgins*] Have I said anything I oughtn't?

MRS HIGGINS [*interposing*] Not at all, Miss Doolittle.

LIZA Well, that's a mercy, anyhow. [*Expansively*] What I always say is —

HIGGINS [*rising and looking at his watch*] Ahem!

LIZA [*looking round at him; taking the hint; and rising*] Well: I must go. [*They all rise. Freddy goes to the door*]. So pleased to have met you. Goodbye. [*She shakes hands with Mrs Higgins*].

MRS HIGGINS Goodbye.

LIZA Goodbye, Colonel Pickering.

PICKERING Goodbye, Miss Doolittle. [*They shake hands*].

LIZA [*nodding to the others*] Goodbye, all.

FREDDY [*opening the door for her*] Are you walking across the Park, Miss Doolittle? If so —

LIZA [*perfectly elegant diction*] Walk! Not bloody likely. [*Sensation*]. I am going in a taxi. [*She goes out*].

Writing

Either

Write a short account of an interview for a job when the applicant has a very working-class accent *or* a very upper-class accent *or* a strong regional accent (Scottish, Yorkshire etc.)

...... and this accent is probably going to cost him/her the job.

Or

Discuss why *you* worry about *your* accent.

The Upper Classes

Extract from *Sunset at Blandings*
by P. G. Wodehouse

Uncles occasionally find their nephews trying and are inclined to compare them to their disadvantage with the young men they knew when they were young men, but it is a very rare uncle who is unable to fraternize with his nieces. And of all his many nieces Gally was fondest of Vicky. She was pretty, a girl whom it was a pleasure to take to race meetings and garden parties, and she had that animation which in his younger days he had found so attractive in music hall artistes and members of the personnel of the chorus.

This animation was missing now. After that tempestuous greeting she had relapsed into a melancholy which would have entitled her to step straight into one of those sombre plays they put on for one performance on Sunday afternoons, and no questions asked. Gally gazed at her, concerned. Beach,* that shrewd diagnostician, had been right, he felt, though his 'somewhat depressed' had been an understatement. Here was plainly a niece whose soul had been passed through the wringer, a niece who had drained the bitter cup and, what is more, had found a dead mouse at the bottom of it. Her demeanour reminded him of a girl he had once taken to Henley Regatta—at the moment when she had discovered that a beetle had fallen down the back of her summer sports wear.

* The family butler

'What on earth's the matter?' he asked.

Nothing.'

Don't be an ass,' said Gally irritably. 'You're obviously as down among the wines and spirits as Mariana at the moated grange.'

'I'm all right, except that I wish I was dead.'

'Were dead, surely,' said Gally, who was a purist. 'What do you want to be dead for? Great Scott!' he exclaimed, suddenly enlightened. 'Have you been jugged? Are you doing a stretch? Is that why you're at Blandings?'

The question did not display such amazing intuition as anyone unfamiliar with Blandings Castle might have supposed. All old English families have their traditions, and the one most rigorously observed in the family to which Vicky belonged ruled that if a young female member of it fell in love with the wrong man she was instantly shipped off to Blandings, there to remain until she came, as the expression was, to her senses.

Young male members who fell in love with the wrong girls were sent to South Africa, as Gally had been thirty years ago. It was all rather unpleasant for the lovelorn juveniles, but better than if they had been living in the Middle Ages, when they would probably have had their heads cut off.

Gally, taking for granted that the reply to his question would be in the affirmative, became reminiscent.

'Lord love a duck,' he said emotionally, 'it seems only yesterday that they had me serving a term in the lowest dungeon below the castle moat because of Dolly Henderson.'

Feminine curiosity momentarily overcame Vicky's depression. She knew vaguely that there had been some sort of trouble with Uncle Gally centuries ago, and she was glad to be about to get the facts.

'Were you imprisoned at Blandings?'

'With gyves upon my wrists.'

'I thought you were sent to South Africa.'

'Later, after I had been well gnawed by rats.'

'Who was Dolly Henderson?'

'Music halls. She sang at the old Oxford and the Tivoli.'

'Tights?'

'Pink. And she was the only woman I ever wanted to marry.'

'Poor Gally.'

'Yes, it was rather a nasty knock when my father bunged a spanner into the works. You never knew him, did you?'

'I met him once when I was a very small child. He paralysed me.'

'I don't wonder. That voice, those bushy eyebrows. You must have thought you were seeing some sinister monster out of a fairy story. Clarence is a great improvement as head of the family. If I told Clarence I wanted to marry somebody, there wouldn't be any family curses and thumping of tables; he would just say "Capital, capital, capital", and that would be that. But don't let's talk about me. Are you very much in love?'

'Yes.'

'What's his name?'

'Jeff Bennison.'

'Any money?'

'No.'

'Which of course makes your stepmother shudder at the sight of him.'

'She's never seen him.'

'But she would shudder if she did. Lack of the stuff is always the rock on which the frail craft of love comes a stinker where Blandings Castle is concerned.'

'And there's another thing.'

'What is that?'

'Jeff's an artist.'

Gally looked grave. To his sister Florence, he knew, an artist would be automatically suspect. *La vie de Bohème,* she would say to herself. Uninhibited goings-on at the Bohemian Ball. Nameless orgies in the old studio. Now more than ever he saw how grievously the cards were stacked against this young couple, and his heart went out to them.

'He started as an architect, but his father lost all his money and he couldn't carry on. So he tried to make a living painting, but you know how it is. Poor darling, he has had to take a job teaching drawing at a girls' school.'

'Good God!'

'Yes, I think that's how he feels about it. Do you mind if I leave you now, Gally? I feel a flood of tears coming on.'

'I am open at the moment to be cried in front of.'

'No, I'd rather be alone.'

'I'm sorry. I was hoping I could do something to cheer you up. But naturally at a time like this you don't want an old gargoyle like me hanging around.'

Gally proceeded on his way, brooding. He would have given much to have been able to do something to brighten life for the unfortunate girl, but no inspiration came beyond a vague determination to speak to his sister Florence like a Dutch uncle, and he was given the opportunity of doing this as he crossed the lawn which led to the Empress's residence. Florence was there, reading a book in the hammock under the big cedar tree which he, though there was no actual ruling on the point, had always looked on as his own property. Many of his deepest thoughts had come to him when on its cushions, and it was with a sense of outrage that he drew up beside it. If people went about pinching one's personal hammock, he felt, what were things coming to?

'Comfortable?' he said.

Florence looked up from her book, expressing no pleasure at seeing him.

'Oh, you're back, Galahad? Did you enjoy yourself in London?'

'Never mind about my enjoying myself in London,' said Gally as sternly as any uncle that ever came out of Holland. 'I've just been talking to Vicky.'

Copy this chart into your book. Then try to complete all ten boxes, listing from the passage ten references that seem to you to establish that the setting, characters, etc. are all upper class. Opposite each item enter your explanation as to why you included that point. A few boxes have been filled in for you.

1 race meetings and garden parties.	I recognise that these activities are part of the upper class social 'round' — Ascot, etc.
2	
3 Henley Regatta	
4	
5	
6	This particular expression is in just the right register I'd associate with the speech of 'toffs'.
7	
8 lawns . . hammock . . cedar tree	Put these together and it suggests. . . . .
9	
10	

Reading (Literature)

'It is a strange thing, but our literature never seems to do more than caricature, parody, distort, misrepresent the classes. And it does not seem to matter which social class we are reading about. It's as if our writers are themselves so much victims of their class they cannot see others honestly, nor themselves clearly.'

On the basis of what you have read in this unit, and any other relevant literature you have enjoyed, say whether you think the above quotation is true or not. Is there any writer you would exempt from this criticism?

Unit 5

Idealism's Other Face

NATIONALISM

From your own experience, listening to the news, reading the paper, you will no doubt have noticed for yourself that what one group calls a 'nationalist' another group calls a 'terrorist' — and this is as good a point as any to start thinking about nationalism.

Belonging is important: to belong to a group means feeling part of it, being accepted and protected by it. There's a strong need to belong in all of us — whether it means belonging to a class, a gang, a team, a family, a community, a nation. Obviously there are some groups we can't choose at all — our families or our countries, for instance. Yet although we may not always approve of them, we often have a deep-rooted loyalty to both. *Why* should this be so?

This unit examines some aspects of *nationalism*. The dictionary defines nationalism as 'patriotic feeling', in other words love of your country. This love can be a powerful force, the inspiration behind many ideas and achievements; it can even develop other ideals, like loyalty, trust, concern, and so on. But there's another side to nationalism. Another dictionary definition of nationalism is the desire for 'the domination of one nation' — in other words, putting that nation ahead of others. Nationalism can sometimes get things out of proportion; it can be used to stir up hatred against other groups; it can be used to reduce people to simple, clear-cut goodies and baddies, heroes and villains, us and them.

So nationalism can inspire great deeds and noble thoughts but it can also create problems, divisions and unhappiness. In this unit we shall examine some of the forms nationalism takes. Before you read the texts try to see what *your* ideas are about nationalism.

Talking

1 To what nation(s) do you belong?

2 Think of an occasion when you, although you are still the same person and British, might prefer to think of yourself as Scottish — English — Welsh — West Indian — Pakistani — Irish — or indeed any sub-division within our multi-cultural society.

3 What makes a nation?

4 Is there such a thing as 'a national character'? If there is, what forms national character?

5 Do you study a foreign language? If so, what do you think is the national character of the people whose language you are learning?

From *The People, Yes*

by Carl Sandburg

A Scotsman keeps the Sabbath and anything else he can lay his hands
    on, say the English.
A fighting Frenchman runs away from even a she-goat, say the
    Germans.
A Russian, say the Poles, can be cheated only by a gypsy, a gypsy by a
    Jew, a Jew by a Greek, and a Greek by the devil.
'If I owned Texas and hell I would rent Texas and move to hell,' said a
    famous general.
'That's right,' wrote a Texas editor: 'Every man for his own country.'
The Peloponnesians pulled these long ago, so did the Russians, the
    Chinese, even the Fijis with rings in their noses.
    Likewise:
An American is an Anglo-Saxon when an Englishman wants some-
    thing from him: or:

When a Frenchman has drunk too much he wants to dance, a German to sing, a Spaniard to gamble, an Italian to brag, an Irishman to fight, an American to make a speech: or:
'What is dumber than a dumb Irishman?' 'A smart Swede.'
These are in all tongues and regions of men. Often they bring laughter and sometimes blood.
The propagandas of hate and war always monkey with the buzz-saw of race and nationality, breed and kin, seldom saying, 'When in doubt hold your tongue.'
In breathing spells of bloody combat between Christian nations the order goes out: 'Don't let the men in the front-line trenches fraternise!'

Reading

1 What two things, in your own words, do the English accuse Scotsmen of?
2 What do the Germans imply about the French?
3 What is the famous general suggesting about Texas?
4 What does the Texas editor's reply suggest?
5 Explain what you understand the expression 'pulled these long ago' to mean.
6 Study the list of races who 'pulled these long ago'; what comments would you offer about that list?
7 What does the word 'likewise' mean here?
8 Explain fully what is meant by the reference to Anglo-Saxon in the next line.
9 What comment does the expression 'A smart Swede' make about Swedes?
10 Explain in your own words what the poet means when he says 'Often they bring laughter and sometimes blood'?
11 Justify the poet's use of 'propagandas', 'monkey' and 'buzz-saw.'
12 What does 'breathing spells' suggest about the activities of Christian nations? And what is the link between Christian nations and 'fraternise' in the last line?

Talking

This poem consists largely of racial jokes.
Discuss, in small groups,

1 the link between racial jokes and stereotypes,
2 the link between stereotypes and prejudice,
3 How do stereotypes influence our views of other nations?
4 How do they influence views of our own nation?

Reading

Love, they say, is blind! And love of country is as blind as any other sort of love.
In the following extract, set in the middle of the nineteenth century, Mr

Podsnap, in Charles Dickens' *Our Mutual Friend*, is waiting for guests to arrive before a dinner party, and is forced to make polite conversation with a visitor from abroad —

Extract from *Our Mutual Friend*
by Charles Dickens

The Unfortunately-Born Foreigner

As a delicate concession to this unfortunately-born foreigner, Mr Podsnap, in receiving him, had presented his wife as 'Madame Podsnap'; also his daughter as 'Mademoiselle Podsnap', with some inclination to add 'ma fille', in which bold venture, however, he checked himself. The Veneerings being at that time the only other arrivals, he had added (in a condescendingly explanatory manner) 'Monsieur Vey-nair-reeng', and had then subsided into English.

'How Do You Like London?' Mr Podsnap now inquired from his station of host, as if he were administering something in the nature of a powder or potion to the deaf child; 'London, Londres, London?'

The foreign gentleman admired it.

'You find it Very Large?' said Mr Podsnap, spaciously.

The foreign gentleman found it very large.

'And Very Rich?'

The foreign gentleman found it, without doubt, enormement riche.

'Enormously Rich, We Say, 'returned Mr Podsnap, in a condescending manner. 'Our English adverbs do Not terminate in Mong and We Pronounce the "ch" as if there were a "t" before it. We Say Ritch.'

'Reetch,' remarked the foreign gentleman.

'And Do You Find, Sir,' pursued Mr Podsnap, with dignity, 'Many Evidences that Strike You, of our British Constitution in the Streets Of The World's Metropolis, London, Londres, London?'

The foreign gentleman begged to be pardoned, but he did not altogether understand.

'The Constitution Britannique,' Mr Podsnap explained, as if he were teaching in an infant school. 'We Say British, But You Say Britannique, You Know' (forgivingly, as if that were not his fault). 'The Constitution, Sir.'

The foreign gentleman said, 'Mais, yees; I know eem.'

A youngish, sallowish gentleman in spectacles, with a lumpy forehead, seated in a supplementary chair at a corner of the table, here caused a profound sensation by saying, in a raised voice, 'ESKER,' and then stopping dead.

'Mais oui', said the foreign gentleman, turning towards him. 'Est-ce que? Quoi donc?'

But the gentleman with the lumpy forehead having for the time delivered himself of all that he found behind his lumps, spake for the time no more.

'I Was Inquiring,' said Mr Podsnap, resuming the thread of his discourse, 'Whether You Have Observed in our Streets as We should say, Upon our Pavvy as You would say, any Tokens—'

The foreign gentleman with patient courtesy entreated pardon; 'But what was tokenz?'

'Marks,' said Mr Podsnap; 'Signs, you know, Appearances—Traces.'

'Ah! Of a Orse?' inquired the foreign gentleman.

'We call it Horse,' said Mr Podsnap, with forbearance. 'In England, Angleterre, England, We Aspirate the "H", and We Say "Horse". Only our Lower Classes Say "Orse"!'

'Pardon,' said the foreign gentleman, 'I am alwiz wrong!'

'Our Language,' said Mr Podsnap, with a gracious consciousness of being always right, 'is Difficult. Ours is a Copious Language, and Trying to Strangers. I will not Pursue my Question.'

But the lumpy gentleman, unwilling to give it up, again madly said, 'ESKER,' and again spake no more.

'It merely referred,' Mr Podsnap explained, with a sense of meritorious proprietorship, 'to Our Constitution, Sir. We Englishmen are Very Proud of our Constitution, Sir. It Was Bestowed Upon Us By Providence. No Other Country is so Favoured as This Country.'

'And ozer countries—?' the foreign gentleman was beginning, when Mr Podsnap put him right again.

'We do not say Ozer; we say Other: the letters are "T" and "H". You say Tay and Aish, You know;' (still with clemency). 'The sound is "th"—"th"!'

'And *other* countries,' said the foreign gentleman. 'They do how?'

'They do, Sir,' returned Mr Podsnap, gravely shaking his head, 'they do—I am sorry to be obliged to say it—*as* they do.'

'It was a little particular of Providence,' said the foreign gentleman, laughing, 'for the frontier is not large.'

'Undoubtedly,' assented Mr Podsnap; 'But So it is. It was the Charter of the Land. This island was Blest, Sir, to the Direct Exclusion of such Other Countries as—as there may happen to be. And if we were all Englishmen present, I would say,' added Mr Podsnap, looking round upon his compatriots, and sounding solemnly with his theme, 'that there is in the Englishman a combination of qualities, a modesty, an independence, a responsibility, a repose, combined with an absence of everything calculated to call a blush into the cheek of a young person, which one would seek in vain among the Nations of the Earth.'

Having delivered this little summary, Mr Podsnap's face flushed, as he thought of the remote possibility of its being at all qualified by any prejudiced citizen of any other country; and, with his favourite right-arm flourish, he put the rest of Europe and the whole of Asia, Africa, and America nowhere.

1 Think of three good words that describe how the foreigner is treated by Mr Podsnap.
2 What is 'the Constitution'? Why are there so many capital letters in Mr Podsnap's speech?
3 What is Mr Podsnap's general view of England? Find evidence to support your answer.
4 What is Mr Podsnap's attitude to other nations? Again, find evidence to support your answer.
5 Why does the young man occasionally interrupt? Why doesn't he continue?
6 What is the foreigner's reaction to Mr Podsnap's claim that 'No Other Country is so Favoured as This Country'?

7 What is the writer's attitude to Mr Podsnap's opinions? Find evidence to support your opinion.

8 What is *your* opinion of Mr Podsnap?
What do you think of his views about: a) his own country, b) foreigners?

Writing

Write a short play script in which a *modern* character, not unlike Mr Podsnap, explains the benefits of his country to a foreigner with a limited grasp of the English language.

Extract from *The Sporting Spirit*
by George Orwell

I am always amazed when I hear people saying that sport creates goodwill between the nations, and that if only the common peoples of the world could meet one another at football or cricket, they would have no inclination to meet on the battlefield. Even if one didn't know from concrete examples (the 1936 Olympic Games, for instance) that international sporting contests lead to orgies of hatred, one could deduce it from general principles.

Nearly all the sports practised nowadays are competitive. You play to win, and the game has little meaning unless you do your utmost to win. On the village green, where you pick up sides and no feeling of local patriotism is involved, it is possible to play simply for the fun and exercise: but as soon as the question of prestige arises, as soon as you feel that you and some larger unit will be disgraced if you lose, the most savage combative instincts are aroused. Anyone who has played even in a school football match knows this. At the international level sport is frankly mimic warfare. But the significant thing is not the behaviour of the players but the attitude of the spectators: and, behind the spectators, of the nations who work themselves into furies over these absurd contests, and seriously believe —at any rate for short periods—that running, jumping and kicking a ball are tests of national virtue.

Even a leisurely game like cricket, demanding grace rather than strength, can cause much ill-will, as we saw in the controversy over body-line bowling and over the rough tactics of the Australian team that visited England in 1921. Football, a game in which everyone gets hurt and every nation has its own style of play which seems unfair to foreigners, is far worse. Worst of all is boxing. One of the most horrible sights in the world is a fight between white and coloured boxers before a mixed audience. But a boxing audience is always disgusting, and the behaviour of the women, in particular, is such that the Army, I believe, does not allow them to attend its contests. At any rate, two or three years ago, when Home Guards and regular troops were holding a boxing tournament, I was placed on guard at the door of the hall, with orders to keep the women out.

In England, the obsession with sport is bad enough, but even fiercer passions are aroused in young countries where game-playing and nationalism are both recent developments. In countries like India or Burma, it is necessary at football matches to have strong cordons of police to keep the crowd from invading the field. In Burma, I have seen the supporters of one side break through the police and disable the goalkeeper of the opposing side at a critical moment. The first big football match that was played in Spain about fifteen years ago, led to an uncontrollable riot. As soon as strong feelings of rivalry are aroused, the notion of playing the game according to the rules always vanishes. People want to see one side on top and the other side humiliated and they forget that victory gained through cheating or through the intervention of the crowd is meaningless. Even when the spectators don't intervene physically they try to influence the name by cheering their own side and "rattling" opposing players with boos and insults. Serious sport has nothing to do with fair play. It is bound up with hatred, jealousy, boastfulness, disregard of all rules and sadistic pleasure in witnessing violence: in other words it is war minus the shooting.

Instead of blah-blahing about the clean, healthy rivalry of the football field and the great part played by the Olympic Games in bringing the nations together, it is more useful to inquire how and why this modern cult of sport arose. Most of the games we now play are of ancient origin, but sport does not seem to have been taken very seriously between Roman times and the nineteenth century. Even in the English public schools the games cult did not start till the later part of the last century. Dr. Arnold, generally regarded as the founder of the modern public school, looked on games as simply a waste of time. Then, chiefly in England and the United States, games were built up into a heavily-financed activity, capable of attracting vast crowds and rousing savage passions, and the infection spread from country to country. It is the most violently combative sports, football and boxing, that have spread the widest. There cannot be much doubt that the whole thing is bound up with the rise of nationalism—that is, with the lunatic modern habit of identifying oneself with large power units and seeing everything in terms of competitive prestige. Also, organized games are more likely to flourish in urban communities where the average human being lives a sedentary or at least a confined life, and does not get much opportunity for creative labour. In a rustic community a boy or young man works off a good deal of his surplus energy by walking, swimming, snowballing, climbing trees, riding horses, and by various sports involving cruelty to animals, such as fishing, cock-fighting and ferreting for rats. In a big town one must indulge in group activities if one wants an outlet for one's physical strength or for one's sadistic impulses. Games are taken seriously in London and New York, and they were taken seriously in Rome and Byzantium: in the Middle Ages they were played, and probably played with much physical brutality, but they were not mixed up with politics nor a cause of group hatreds.

If you wanted to add to the vast fund of ill-will existing in the world at this moment, you could hardly do it better than by a series of football matches between Jews and Arabs, Germans and Czechs, Indians and British, Russians and Poles, and Italians and Yugoslavs, each match to be watched by a mixed audience of 100,000 spectators. I do not, of course, suggest that sport is one of the main causes of international rivalry; big-scale sport is itself, I think, merely another effect of the causes that have produced nationalism. Still, you do make things worse by sending forth a team of eleven men, labelled as national champions, to do battle against some rival team, and allowing it to be felt on all sides that whichever nation is defeated will "lose face".

Reading

1 In what ways, according to Orwell, do *commercialism* and *nationalism* interfere with the idealistic aims of sport?

2 'At the international level sport is frankly mimic warfare.'
'(Serious) sport is war minus the shooting.'
Explain why you feel that Orwell's attitude here is fair or unfair.

3 Choose from the passage three references that seem to you to 'date' this essay, make it seem a bit old-fashioned.

4 In your own words, write down one of Orwell's ideas or observations about international sport that still seems to you correct and justified.

5 What was Orwell's explanation as to why some sports were worse than others for developing ill-will?

6 Is there, in your view, a positive side to international sport that Orwell has chosen to ignore?

Reading (Literature)

'You can agree with Orwell — or disagree with him: but you have to admit, the man writes with *vigour*'.
Write a short essay, with this as your text. Indicate briefly whether, in general, you agree or disagree with Orwell's argument in *The Sporting Spirit*, then try to explain, by quotation and reference, what you understand by 'vigour'.

But strong feelings for one's country can produce very idealistic statements, full of warmth and love. Look at the two poems that follow.

Home-Thoughts, From Abroad

by Robert Browning

Oh, to be in England
Now that April's there,
And whoever wakes in England
Sees, some morning, unaware,
That the lowest boughs and the brushwood sheaf
Round the elm-tree bole are in tiny leaf,
While the chaffinch sings on the orchard bough
In England — now!

And after April, when May follows,
And the whitethroat builds, and all the swallows!
Hark, where my blossomed pear-tree in the hedge
Leans to the field and scatters on the clover
Blossoms and dewdrops — at the bent spray's edge —
That's the wise thrush; he sings each song twice over,
Lest you should think he never could recapture
The first fine careless rapture!
And though the fields look rough with hoary dew,
All will be gay when noontide wakes anew
The buttercups, the little children's dower
— Far brighter than this gaudy melon-flower!

Reading

1 In which season is the poet writing?

2 Choose two details from the first verse which particularly appeal to the poet.

3 Choose an expression from the first verse which indicates the poet's mood, and explain how it does so.

4 Select two details from the second verse which add to the poet's picture of England. Explain how they add to that picture.

5 What do we learn about the location and climate of the poet's present situation from the last line?

6 What is his attitude to this situation?

7 How might this influence the way he sees England?

8 How complete and accurate is the description of England in this poem?

The Soldier

by Rupert Brooke

If I should die, think only this of me:
That there's some corner of a foreign field
That is forever England. There shall be
In that rich earth a richer dust concealed:
A dust whom England bore, shaped, made aware,
Gave, once, her flowers to love, her ways to roam,
A body of England's, breathing English air,
Washed by the rivers, blest by suns of home.

And think, this heart, all evil shed away,
A pulse in the eternal mind, no less
Gives somewhere back the thoughts by England given;
Her sights and sounds; dreams happy as her day;
And laughter, learnt of friends; and gentleness,
In hearts at peace, under an English heaven.

November–December 1914

Note: This poem is written in the *sonnet* form. A sonnet is like a coin — small and carefully designed. It is only fourteen lines long and has a regular beat and rhyme pattern (work out the beat by humming the lines! Work out the rhyme pattern of this particular sonnet by looking at the last word of each line). Very often, just like a coin, it will have two sides to it: the *octet*, or first eight lines, and the *sestet*, the last six. Where there's a shift in ideas — where the coin is flipped over — is known as the *volta*. Just like most coins, there's a different picture on the other side.

Talking

1 This sonnet, as the title suggests, is about the prospect of dying for your country during a war. Is it a war poem?

2 How many times does 'England'/'English' appear in the poem? Why do you think this is so?

3 In a way, the poem reads like the poet's personal will. Why has he listed these particular items?

4 Look at the structure of this sonnet. In what ways do the ideas of the *octet* differ from those in the *sestet*?

Reading

1 Look at the poet's word choice.
When we don't dwell on the more unpleasant aspects of experience, when we describe things unpleasant or offensive by milder, less disturbing expressions, we are using *euphemism*.
In the octet, how is the poet's possible death described and made more acceptable?

2 How is England made to seem attractive and why?

3 How does Brooke's description of England differ from Browning's in the previous poem?

4 Is Brooke's nationalism similar to Browning's? What do you think of the ardent patriotism found in both poems?

Here's a slightly different presentation of what it means to give your life for your country. This extract comes from *Sunset Song* by Lewis Grassic Gibbon.

Extract from *Sunset Song*

by Lewis Grassic Gibbon

Snow was shining in the Grampians, far in the coarse hills there, and it wouldn't be long ere the dark came. Syne at last the minister was seen coming up, he'd on the bit robes that he hardly ever wore, Chris Tavendale walked by the side of him and behind was a third childe that nobody knew, a Highlander in kilts and with pipes on his shoulder, great and red-headed, who could he be? And then Ellison minded, he said the man had been friend to young Ewan Tavendale, he'd been the best man at Ewan's marriage, McIvor his name was.

The minister held open the gate for Chris and through it she came, all clad in her black, young Ewan's hand held fast in hers, he'd grown fair like his father, the bairn, dark-like and solemn he was. Chris's face was white and solemn as well except when she looked at the minister as he held the gate open, it was hardly decent the look that she gave him, they might keep their courting till the two were alone. Folk cried *Ay, minister!* and he cried back cheerily and went striding to the midst of the old stone circle, John Brigson was standing there with his hands on the strings that held the bit clout.

The minister said, *Let us pray*, and folk took off their hats, it smote cold on your pow. The sun was fleering up in the clouds, it was quiet on the hill, you saw young

Chris stand looking down on Kinraddie with her bairn's hand in hers. And then the Lord's Prayer was finished, the minister was speaking just ordinary, he said they had come to honour the folk whom the War had taken, and that the clearing of this ancient site was maybe the memory that best they'd have liked. And he gave a nod to old Brigson and the strings were pulled and off came the clout and there on the Standing Stone the words shone out in their dark grey lettering, plain and short:

FOR : THE : MEMORY : OF :
CHARLES : STRACHAN : JAMES :
LESLIE : ROBERT : DUNCAN :
EWAN : TAVENDALE : WHO :
WERE : OF : THIS : LAND : AND :
FELL : IN : THE : GREAT : WAR :
IN : FRANCE :
REVELATION : II CH : 28 VERSE

And then, with the night waiting out by on Blawearie brae, and the sun just verging the coarse hills, the minister began to speak again, his short hair blowing in the wind that had come, his voice not decent and a kirk-like bumble, but ringing out over the loch:

FOR I WILL GIVE YOU THE MORNING STAR

In the sunset of an age and an epoch we may write that for epitaph of the men who were of it. They went quiet and brave from the lands they loved, though seldom of that love might they speak, it was not in them to tell in words of the earth that moved and lived and abided, their life and enduring love. And who knows at the last what memories of it were with them, the springs and the winters of this land

and all the sounds and scents of it that had once been theirs, deep, and a passion of their blood and spirit, those four who died in France? With them we may say there died a thing older then themselves, these were the Last of the Peasants, the last of the Old Scots folk. A new generation comes up that will know them not, except as a memory in a song, they passed with the things that seemed good to them with loves and desires that grow dim and alien in the days to be. It was the old Scotland that perished then, and we may believe that never again will the old speech and the old songs, the old curses and the old benedictions, rise but with alien effort to our lips.

The last of the peasants, those four that you knew, took that with them to the darkness and the quietness of the places where they sleep. And the land changes, their parks and their steadings are a desolation where the sheep are pastured, we are told that great machines come soon to till the land, and the great herds come to feed on it, the crofter has gone, the man with the house and the steading of his own and the land closer to his heart than the flesh of his body. Nothing, it has been said, is true but change, nothing abides, and here in Kinraddie where we watch the building of those little prides and those little fortunes on the ruins of the little farms we must give heed that these also do not abide, that a new spirit shall come to the land with the greater herd and the great machines. For greed of place and possession and great estate those four had little head, the kindness of friends and the warmth of toil and the peace of rest—they asked no more from God or man, and no less would they endure.

So, lest we shame them, let us believe that the new oppressions and foolish greeds are no more than mists that pass. They died for a world that is past, these men, but they did not die for this that we seem to inherit. Beyond it and us there shines a greater hope and a newer world, undreamt when these four died. But we doubt which side the battle they would range themselves did they live to-day, need we doubt the answer they cry to us even now, the four of them, from the places of the sunset?

And then, as folk stood dumbfounded, this was just sheer politics, plain what he meant, the Highland man McIvor tuned up his pipes and began to step slow round the stone circle by Blawearie Loch, slow and quiet, and folk watched him, the dark was near, it lifted your hair and was eerie and uncanny, the *Flowers of the Forest* as he played it.

It rose and rose and wept and cried, that crying for the men that fell in battle, and there was Kirsty Strachan weeping quietly and others with her, and the young ploughmen they stood with glum, white faces, they'd no understanding or caring, it was something that vexed and tore at them, it belonged to times they had no knowing of.

Reading

1 The setting of a piece of writing — where *and* when the action happens — can be very important.
What is the setting of this incident? Find evidence from the first three paragraphs. Why are the people gathered at this spot? When? Why?

2 Some of the language used is not standard English. Pick out five examples from the first three paragraphs and explain what they mean.

3 Why has the writer chosen to write in this fashion?

4 The minister uses several rhetorical devices to make his speech more powerful. Quote an example of repetition, climax and antithesis.

5 Look carefully at the minister's speech.
   a) What kind of men, according to him, were the people he mentions?
   b) What was their attitude to the land?
   c) What does the minister say about the nature of the old life and the nature of the new?
   d) What, according to the minister, would have been the men's attitude to the present — and why?

6 How do the people there react to the minister's speech?

7 How does the music influence their response?

8 What relationship do you see between the minister's speech and the title of the novel?

Reading (Literature)

Compare the forms of nationalism in this piece of writing with those in the two preceding poems. How far does the language used in each text suit its 'patriotic feeling'?

Nationalism, patriotic enthusiasm, as we have seen, often is based on a strong sense of one's history, of the past. Compared with the past, the present has a habit of proving disappointing!

The following extract is from Shakespeare's *Richard II*. It is spoken by John of Gaunt, an old nobleman on his deathbed. No one can doubt the sincerity of his attachment to his country — but he is saddened by its condition at the time when the action of the play occurs (near the end of the fourteenth century).

Extract from *Richard II*
by William Shakespeare

This royal throne of kings, this sceptered isle,
This earth of majesty, this seat of Mars,
This other Eden, demi-paradise,
This fortress built by nature for herself
Against infection and the hand of war,
This happy breed of men, this little world,
This precious stone set in the silver sea,
Which serves it in the office of a wall,
Or as a moat defensive to a house,
Against the envy of less happier lands;
This blessed plot, this earth, this realm, this England
This nurse, this teeming womb of royal kings,
Feared by their breed, and famous by their birth,
Renowned for their deeds as far from home,

For Christian service and true chivalry,
As is the sepulchre in stubborn Jewry
Of the world's ransom, blessed Mary's Son:
This land of such dear souls, this dear dear land,
Dear for her reputation through the world,
Is now leased out — I die pronouncing it —
Like to a tenement of pelting[1] farm.
England, bound in with the triumphant sea,
Whose rocky shore beats back the envious siege
Of wat'ry Neptune, is now bound in with shame,
With inky blots, and rotten parchment bonds:
That England, that was wont to conquer others,
Hath made a shameful conquest of itself:
Ah, would the scandal vanish with my life,
How happy then were my ensuing death!

[1] paltry

Talking

In small groups, look closely at the speech and discuss these questions which deal with its *ideas*.

1 What natural advantages does the land have?

2 What qualities could (and should) its rulers possess?

3 Pick an expression which describes the people of the island. What is John of Gaunt's opinion of them?

4 In your own words explain why John of Gaunt is saddened.

5 What is his final wish?

6 What is your opinion of the views he expresses?

Reading

Look closely at the speech, examining its *language* and *structure*, before answering the following questions.

1 Look at lines 1–17. What rhetorical devices does John of Gaunt use to emphasise the various qualities of the island?

2 Choose five expressions which suggest England's pleasantness and nobility. Explain briefly how the expressions achieve this effect.

Writing

Although the language may be unfamiliar, the ideas set out by John of Gaunt are not. Write a speech along similar lines by a character living in modern times, choosing an appropriate country and situation for him/her.
Try to use some of the devices found in this speech, though feel free to use others too.

In a similar way the Scottish poet Edwin Muir expressed his discontent with the present as compared with the past, seeing a loss of continuity, tradition, etc. as weakening a nation's sense of identity.

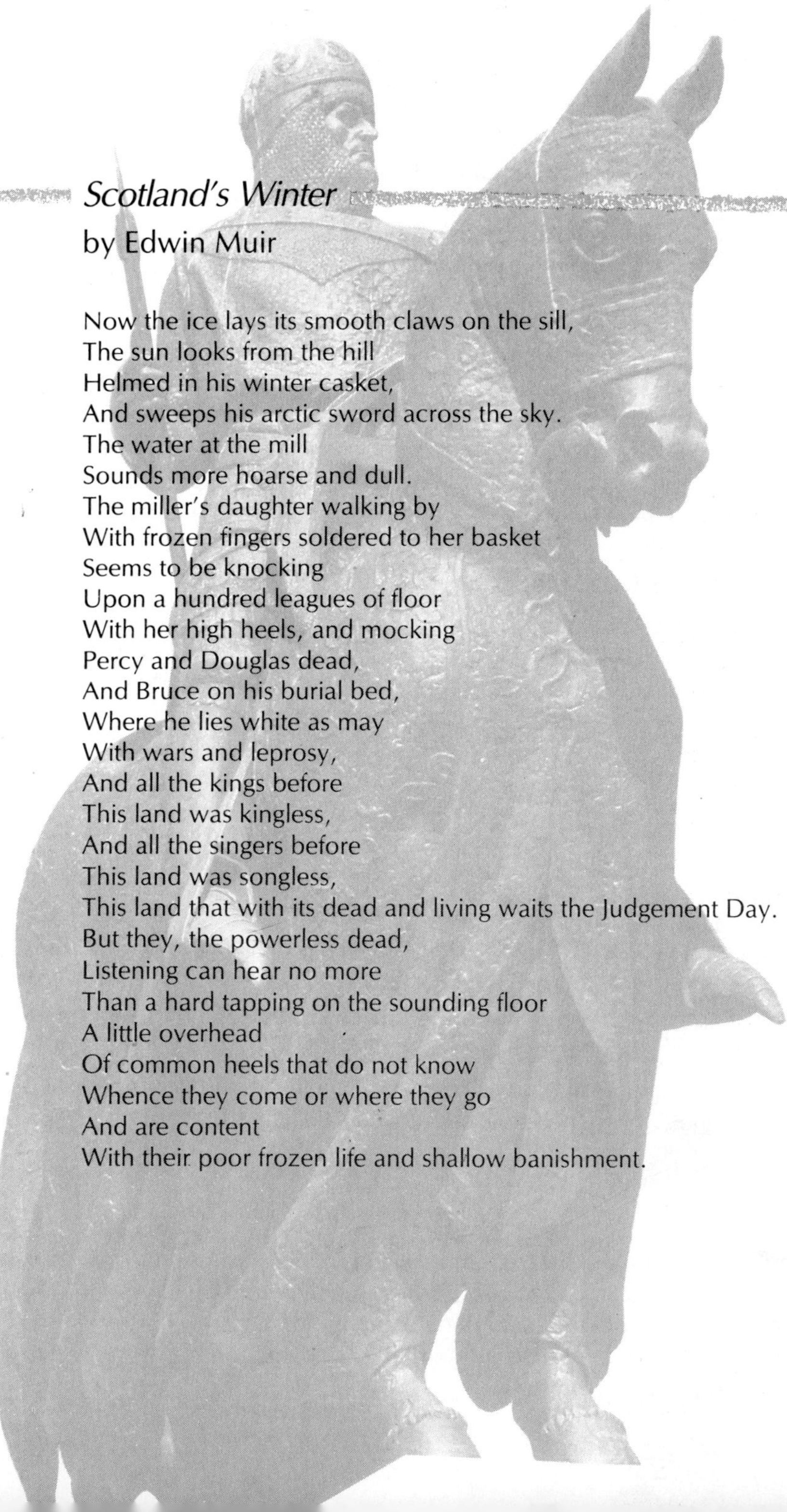

Scotland's Winter

by Edwin Muir

Now the ice lays its smooth claws on the sill,
The sun looks from the hill
Helmed in his winter casket,
And sweeps his arctic sword across the sky.
The water at the mill
Sounds more hoarse and dull.
The miller's daughter walking by
With frozen fingers soldered to her basket
Seems to be knocking
Upon a hundred leagues of floor
With her high heels, and mocking
Percy and Douglas dead,
And Bruce on his burial bed,
Where he lies white as may
With wars and leprosy,
And all the kings before
This land was kingless,
And all the singers before
This land was songless,
This land that with its dead and living waits the Judgement Day.
But they, the powerless dead,
Listening can hear no more
Than a hard tapping on the sounding floor
A little overhead
Of common heels that do not know
Whence they come or where they go
And are content
With their poor frozen life and shallow banishment.

Reading

1 An *image*, you remember, is the picture we get from the writer's use of words. At times this picture is not strictly speaking (literally) true but still helps to present a certain idea. Explain the image used in lines 2–4, commenting on its appropriateness to the overall idea of the poem.

2 Explain the image and its intended effect in–
  (a) 'Now the ice lays its smooth claws on the sill'.
  (b) 'With frozen fingers soldered to her basket'.

3 Why does the poet use the expression 'a hundred leagues of floor'? What idea is conveyed by it?

4 In what way can 'this land' be described as 'kingless' and 'songless'?

5 What single word from the poem indicates the miller's daughter's attitude to her ancestral land?

6 Look carefully at the concluding eight lines. What comment is the poet making about: a) the dead Scots, b) the living Scots?

7 Comment on the appropriateness of the title.

8 What is the significance of the names Percy, Douglas and Bruce to: a) the poet, b) the miller's daughter, c) to you?

Writing

Having read the material in this unit and discussed the different aspects of nationalism you should be able to deal with these writing tasks:

1 'Your country needs you!'
How far do you need your country?
Or any country? Is nationalism necessary or desirable at all?

2 'My country, 'tis of thee,
Sweet land of liberty,
Of thee I sing.'
Write an account of your country which reflects the mood of this quotation or, if you feel more critical of your country, write an account of those things which you like and dislike about your country.

3 'O wad some Pow'r the giftie gie us
To see oursels as others see us!' (Robert Burns)
Write an account of aspects of your country — language, culture, customs, social behaviour, for example — as an outsider might see them. You might wish to use a light-hearted tone.

4 'Patriotism is the last refuge of a scoundrel' (Dr Johnson)
Discuss this statement, explaining what it means and how far you agree with it.

5 Write a commentary on a sporting occasion where you are *supposed* to be neutral but where your nationalistic bias becomes more obvious as the action develops.

Unit 6

New Ideals for Old

WAR

Why do we have wars?

Reasons, I suppose, are as plentiful as blackberries. Try to list half a dozen.

Among all the other reasons — economic, religious, psychological — consider two others:
that we want to defend our ideals from attack,
that we want others to accept our ideals.

Or is all talk of ideals being involved in war simply a cover for the real reasons, or an attempt to disguise the horror and brutality of war — even from ourselves?

Anyhow, one thing you will discover: in the course of the war itself, we find that the conflict creates its own ideals — like bravery, sacrifice, discipline.

All of which might suggest not so much that we just swap ideals in a thoughtless manner — but that, whatever our situation, we feel the need for some sort of ideal.

What causes war?

Here is an extract from *Gulliver's Travels* by Jonathan Swift (1667–1745). Here, Gulliver is in the land of the Houyhnhnms (get your teacher to say it!). The Houyhnhnms are a race remarkably like horses and characterised by a good nature. In the same land are other creatures called Yahoos, remarkably like men and characterised by a violent and primitive nature. Gulliver is keen to explain the glories of European civilisation to a Houyhnhnm. He gets round to the subject of war — and nothing seems to have changed very much.

Extract from *Gulliver's Travels*
by Jonathan Swift

He asked me what were the usual causes or motives that made one country go to war with another. I answered they were innumerable; but I should only mention a few of the chief. Sometimes the ambition of princes, who never think they have land or people enough to govern; sometimes the corruption of ministers, who engage their master in a war in order to stifle or divert the clamour of the subjects against their evil administration. Difference in opinions hath cost many millions of lives: for instance, whether flesh be bread, or bread be flesh; whether the juice of a certain berry be blood or wine; whether whistling be a vice or a virtue; whether it be better to kiss a post, or throw it into the fire; what is the best colour for a coat, whether black, white, red, or gray; and whether it should be long or short, narrow or wide, dirty or clean; with many more. Neither are any wars so furious and bloody, or of so long continuance, as those occasioned by difference in opinion, especially if it be in things indifferent.

Sometimes the quarrel between two princes is to decide which of them shall dispossess a third of his dominions, where neither of them pretend to any right. Sometimes one prince quarrelleth with another, for fear the other should quarrel with him. Sometimes a war is entered upon, because the enemy is too strong, and sometimes because he is too weak. Sometimes our neighbours want the things which we have, or have the things which we want; and we both fight, till they take ours or give us theirs. It is a very justifiable cause of a war to invade a country after the people have been wasted by famine, destroyed by pestilence, or embroiled by factions among themselves. It is justifiable to enter into war against our nearest ally, when one of his towns lies convenient for us, or a territory of land, that would render our dominions round and complete. If a prince sends forces into a nation, where the people are poor and ignorant, he may lawfully put half of them to death, and make slaves of the rest, in order to civilize and reduce them from their barbarous way of living. It is a very kingly, honourable and frequent practice, when one prince desires the assistance of another to secure him against an invasion, that the assistant, when he hath driven out the invader, should seize on the dominions himself, and kill, imprison, or banish the prince he came to relieve. Alliance by blood or marriage is a frequent cause of war between princes; and the nearer the kindred is, the greater is their disposition to quarrel: poor nations are hungry, and rich nations are proud; and pride and hunger will ever be at variance. For these reasons, the trade of a soldier is held the most honourable of all others; because a soldier is a *Yahoo* hired to kill in cold blood as many of his own species, who have never offended him, as possibly he can.

What you have told me (said my master), upon the subject of war, does indeed discover most admirably the effects of that reason you pretend to: however, it is happy that the shame is greater than the danger; and that nature hath left you utterly uncapable of doing much mischief.

For your mouths lying flat with your faces, you can hardly bite each other to any purpose, unless by consent. Then as to the claws upon your feet before and behind, they are so short and tender, that one of our *Yahoos* would drive a dozen of yours before him. And therefore in recounting the numbers of those who have been killed in battle, I cannot but think that you have *said the thing which is not.*

I could not forbear shaking my head, and smiling a little at his ignorance. And being no stranger to the art of war, I gave him a description of cannons, culverins, muskets, carabines, pistols, bullets, powder, swords, bayonets, battles, sieges, retreats, attacks, undermines, countermines, bombardments, sea fights; ships sunk with a thousand men, twenty thousand killed on each side; dying groans, limbs flying in the air, smoke, noise, confusion, trampling to death under horses' feet; flight, pursuit, victory; fields strewed with carcases left for food to dogs, and wolves, and birds of prey; plundering, stripping, ravishing, burning and destroying. And to set forth the valour of my own dear countrymen, I assured him, that I had seen them blow up a hundred enemies at once in a siege, and as many in a ship, and beheld the dead bodies come down in pieces from the clouds, to the great diversion of the spectators.

I was going on to more particulars, when my master commanded me silence. He said, whoever understood the nature of *Yahoos* might easily believe it possible for so vile an animal to be capable of every action I had named, if their strength and cunning equalled their malice.

Reading

Paragraph 1

1 What three main reasons does Gulliver give for going to war?

2 How does the list of seemingly petty disputes influence the reader's attitude to war?

3 The writer is mocking certain disputes — what do you think these disputes really are?

Paragraph 2

4 How is a soldier defined? Do you think this is a fair definition?

Paragraphs 3 and 4

5 Why is the Houyhnhnm puzzled by Gulliver's account?

6 What is 'the thing which is not'? Why do you think the Houyhnhnm calls it by this and not its proper name?

Paragraph 5

7 What does Gulliver *intend* by supplying the list of different methods of destruction? What does he *actually* achieve?

8 When a writer gives us a piece of information which *on the surface* seems his view but in reality is the opposite he is being *ironic*.
Irony is the use of an expression which says one thing but is *intended* to say the opposite.
How does Swift indicate that Gulliver's account is to be taken ironically?

The two poems which follow express very different approaches to war — though they were written about the same war.

The Dead

by Rupert Brooke

Blow out, you bugles, over the rich Dead!
There's none of these so lonely and poor of old,
But, dying has made us rarer gifts than gold.
These laid the world away; poured out the red
Sweet wine of youth; gave up the years to be
Of work and joy, and that unhoped serene,
That men call age; and those who would have been,
Their sons, they gave, their immortality.

Blow, bugles, blow! They brought us, for our dearth,
Holiness, lacked so long, and Love, and Pain.
Honour has come back, as a king, to earth,
And paid his subjects with a royal wage;
And Nobleness walks in our ways again;
And we have come into our heritage.

They

by Siegfried Sassoon

The Bishop tells us: 'When the boys come back
'They will not be the same; for they'll have fought
'In a just cause: they lead the last attack
'On Anti-Christ; their comrades' blood has bought
'New right to breed an honourable race,
'They have challenged Death and dared him face to face.'

'We're none of us the same!' the boys reply.
'For George lost both his legs; and Bill's stone blind;
'Poor Jim's shot through the lungs and like to die;
'And Bert's gone syphilitic: you'll not find
'A chap who's served that hasn't found some change.'
And the Bishop said: 'The ways of God are strange!'

Reading

1 In Brooke's poem, what is his attitude to death in battle?

2 How is death described? Pick out a phrase that seems to you to illustrate it.

3 Brooke uses here a great deal of *personification*, the presentation of non-human things as if they were persons. Why does he use this so much?

4 Does Brooke *intend* to give realistic details? If not, what is his intention?

5 Look at Sassoon's poem and the reasons the Bishop gives for going to war. Who is he describing as Anti-Christ and why does he use this term?

6 In what way does the boys' language differ from the Bishop's?

7 What do you think was Sassoon's *main* aim in presenting the views of the Bishop with those of the boys?

8 'The ways of God are strange.' Do you think that the Bishop has changed his views—or is he using his ideals to interpret what he sees? Give a reason.

9 To whom does the *They* of the title refer?

10 Both these poems deal with what might befall soldiers in a war. Which of the two do you find more realistic?
What in your view makes one more realistic and the other less so?

11 Realism isn't everything. Which poem do you actually prefer? Give at least one good reason to support your opinion.

The Death of the Ball Turret Gunner

by Randall Jarrell

From my mother's sleep I fell into the State,
And I hunched in its belly till my wet fur froze.
Six miles from earth, loosed from its dream of life,
I woke to black flak and the nightmare fighters.
When I died they washed me out of the turret with a hose.

This poem is based on a very interesting *image*. Think of words like 'hunched', 'belly', 'wet fur,' for example. What *image* do you get? What other words help to fix the image? Why has the poet chosen this image for this particular poem?

Perhaps in the fury and fear of battle the real reasons for the war are forgotten. Survival may be your greatest objective. And what about the enemy? What do you feel about the man on the other side? Do your feelings change once the fighting's over? Perhaps your enemy isn't so different from yourself after all.

Look at *Vergissmeinnicht* ('Forget Me Not') and try to see why the poet has chosen to describe an *enemy* soldier and why he has chosen to describe him in this particular way.

Vergissmeinnicht

by Keith Douglas

Three weeks gone and the combatants gone
returning over the nightmare ground
we found the place again, and found
the soldier sprawling in the sun.

The frowning barrel of his gun
overshadowing. As we came on
that day, he hit my tank with one
like the entry of a demon.

Look. Here in the gunpit spoil
the dishonoured picture of his girl
who has put: *Steffi. Vergissmeinnicht*
in a copybook gothic script.

We see him almost with content,
abased, and seeming to have paid
and mocked at by his own equipment
that's hard and good when he's decayed.

But she would weep to see today
how on his skin the swart flies move;
the dust upon the paper eye
and the burst stomach like a cave.

For here the lover and killer are mingled
who had one body and one heart.
And death who had the soldier singled
has done the lover mortal hurt.

Reading

1 Briefly explain what this poem is about — consider who is speaking, where and when it takes place as well as what is described.

2 What details make an impression on you? Why do you think this is so? (You might consider *method* of presentation here.)

3 Why do you think the poet concentrates on the physical appearance of the soldier?

4 What are the poet's feelings when he first sees the soldier — supply evidence! Do these feelings change at all? If so *where* and *how* do they change?

5 One of the techniques used in this poem is *contrast* — the positioning of ideas or details to bring out the difference between them.
Find several examples of contrast in the poem which you find effective or interesting. In explaining why you have chosen them, comment on their *intended* purpose.

6 What does the last verse suggest about the nature of man — and, perhaps, about the idealism of love and/or war?
How far do you agree with the poet?

7 Look again at the title — does it have any other meaning than the obvious one? Who might be the 'Me' of 'Forget Me Not'?

Talking

The texts which follow deal with one example of ideals being used to excuse mass murder: the attempt to destroy the European Jews and other racially inferior groups by the Nazis during the Second World War. It is an example of ideals creating a nightmare.

After explaining that the extermination of the Jews — and other apparently inferior racial types — was due in part to deep-rooted fear and hatred, Leo Kuper describes the ruthless efficiency of the murderers:

Extract from *Genocide*
by Leo Kuper

Then there was the extreme bureaucratic organization of the genocide. This was one of its most dehumanised aspects. We know all too well the passionate outbursts by murderous mobs under the incitement of their leaders. These fall well within the expected range of human behaviour. But to use bureaucratic planning and procedures and regulation for a massive operation of systematic murder throughout a whole continent speaks of an almost inconceivably profound dehumanisation. Who would have believed that human beings would send out mobile killing units for the slaughter of unarmed men, women and children in distant lands? Or that they were capable of organising, on the model of a modern industrial plant, killing centres which processed their victims for slaughter, as if on a conveyor belt; eliminated waste, gathered in, with careful inventory, their few possessions, their clothes, gold teeth, women's hair, and regulated the distribution of these relics? Or that the killing centres might be combined with slave camps, in which the exploitation of labour was carried to the extreme of rapid expendability, or that such leading German firms as I. G. Farben and Krupp would establish branches in the vicinity of the gas chambers and crematoria?

Yet all this was done, with co-ordination between the bureaucracies of the state, of the Nazi party, of the military and big business. The civil service infused the other hierarchies with its sure-footed planning and bureaucratic thoroughness. From the army the machinery of destruction acquired its military precision, discipline and callousness. Industry's influence was felt in the great emphasis upon accounting, penny-saving and salvage, as well as in the factory-like efficiency of the killing centres. Finally, the party contributed to the entire apparatus an idealism, a sense of 'mission', and a notion of 'history-making'.

Reading

1 What aspect does Kuper find most distressing about the way the mass murder war carried out?
2 What does the expression 'carried to the extreme of rapid expendability' tell you about the conditions in the slave camps?
3 What is a bureaucracy? How does it add to the process of dehumanisation?
4 What did each of the following bureaucracies add to the machinery of death: a) the state b) the military c) big business d) the Nazi party?
5 What do we mean by 'a sense of mission'? What was the mission?
6 Can you think of occasions when a sense of mission has created happiness?

There are many horrifying accounts of the conditions in the camps. The poem which follows does not dwell on the brutality and physical pain which so many experienced. Nor does it seem angry. But the pain and anger are there if you look closely enough.

Pigtail

by Tadeusz Rosewicz
(translated by A. Czerniawski)

When all the women in the transport
had their heads shaved
four workmen with brooms made of birch twigs
swept up
and gathered up the hair

Behind clean glass
the stiff hair lies
of those suffocated in gas chambers
there are pins and side combs
in this hair

The hair is not shot through with light
is not parted by the breeze
is not touched by any hand
or rain or lips

In huge chests
clouds of dry hair
of those suffocated
and a faded plait
a pigtail with a ribbon
pulled at school
by naughty boys.

Talking

1 This poem deliberately understates the horrors of the concentration camps. What suggests the setting and the fate of the people? What suggests their age and sex?

2 What details does the poet emphasise and why does he do this?

3 Look at the third verse. Comment on the details of the list. Why supply the list at all?
How does this verse contrast with last one?

4 Do you think this poem is more effective *because* it avoids explicit description of violence? Would presenting the full horror have improved it?

In 1945 the world was shocked to learn about the mass murder committed by the Nazis. People said that such horrors must never happen again. After all, these were crimes against humanity. In 1979 John Pilger sent this report from Cambodia:

Dateline Cambodia

DEATH OF A GENTLE PEOPLE . . .

THE PLANE flies low, following the Mekong River west from Vietnam. Once over Cambodia, what we see below us silences everybody on board.

There is nobody, no movement, not even an animal, as if the great population of Asia stopped at the border. Whole towns and villages on the river bank stand empty: the doors of houses flapping open, cars on their side, mangled bicycles in a heap, chairs and beds in the street.

Beside tangled power lines there is the lone shadow of a child, lying or sitting. It does not move.

The endless landscape of South East Asia, the patchwork of rice paddies and fields, is barely discernible; nothing appears to grow except the forest and tall, wild grass. On the rim of large towns this grass will follow straight lines, as if planted; it is fertilised, we later see, by human compost, by the remains of tens of thousands of men, women and children.

All of them murdered.

Cambodia, which I remember as the most gentle and graceful land in all of Asia, a land whose peace in a region of unrelenting war was unique, all but vanished from the headlines four and a half years ago; and what has happened here since has no parallel in modern times.

That may sound a sweeping claim, but it is true. Coming here is like happening on something unimaginable: a human catastrophe and crime without measure. For even Hitler's demonry did not involve the enslavement of the *entire* population and the systematic slaughter of all those "touched" and corrupted by the twentieth century.

Nor did Stalin's terror include the banning of ALL learning, all books, all arts, all music and song, and the abolition of the family and all expressions of joy, love and grief, and the destruction of all machines.

All that has happened in Cambodia.

Out of a world-renowned royal ballet of some 500 dancers, a few dozen survive. Before 1975 there were 550 Cambodian doctors; there are now 48. The statistics are numbing. Cambodia's population in 1975 was roughly seven million. Today, between a million and a half and three million people are "missing," presumed dead.

As we make our final approach into the deserted airport at Phnom Penh, the capital, there is a pyramid of cars, overgrown by the jungle — some of them brand new four years ago — and ambulances and fire engines, and refrigerators, washing machines, hair dryers, generators, typewriters, as if an army of Luddites has tried to sweep them back in time.

Before April 17, 1975, anybody who had owned these things, anybody who had lived in a city or town, was under virtual sentence of death. Anybody with education or a modern skill was killed if their identity was revealed: doctors, teachers, technicians, skilled workers, even schoolchildren; anybody who knew foreigners.

The images also numb. An emaciated child walks alone down the centre of a main boulevard that once was filled with traffic in a capital city that used to hold 2½ million people, gangs of children scavenge in the garbage. They are mostly orphans and many are infants no more than five years old, for few of those born during the period of terror appear to have survived. Young adults are equally difficult to find; a generation has gone. Indeed this is now a nation mostly of children isolated from the world and facing starvation of such intensity that not even a comparison with Biafra is adequate.

Who did this? How could it happen?

In the spring of 1970, Cambodia's tranquility was terminated by the greatest saturation bombing in history. This was the secret war launched by President Nixon and Dr Henry Kissinger in violation of American Constitutional law and in defiance of Congress. Pilots were sworn to secrecy and their operational logs were falsified or destroyed. For three years the American public knew nothing about it.

By 1973 the equivalent, in tons of bombs, of five Hiroshimas had fallen on neutral Cambodia.

The military aim was the destruction of a mythical Vietcong base in Cambodia. President Nixon's aim was to show the Vietnamese communists how "tough" he could be: a policy he once described as the "Madman Theory of War."

The Madman Theory of War threw Cambodia into turmoil; the delicate balance of royalists, republicans and communists of varying shades was destroyed, and Prince Sihanouk, the peacock, jazz-loving ruler who had preserved this balance, was overthrown by the military.

In the forests, a small group of fanatics, whom the Prince had called the Khmer Rouge and who were inspired by the maniac Red Guards of China's "cultural revolution" in the 1960s, intensified their revolution.

They declared 1975 Year Zero, literally the beginning of the end of the modern world. The ideological aim of their revolution was to recreate a "pure" rural society, "classless and glorious", similar to that of the Khmer empire of the tenth century. Because there were so few of them — they represented

probably no more than 10 per cent of the people—this meant controlling the population by enslaving it and reducing it by half.

. . . . When the Vietnamese army drove into Phnom Penh last January, ending four and a half years of terror, they found the city almost exactly as it had been abandoned on the first day of Year Zero.

It is a haunting, unforgettable sight. In the silent, airless humidity, it is like entering a city the size of Manchester, without people, as if in the wake of a nuclear war which spared only the buildings.

Houses, flats, office blocks, the university, schools, hotels are deserted and open as they were left when more than two million people were marched away at gunpoint, most of them to their death.

A medical diploma lies trampled on a front path; a tricycle is crushed in the gutter; traffic lights are jammed at red. Except in the centre, there is no electricity. There is neither sewerage nor drinking water; the drains and reservoirs remain polluted with bodies.

The barbarism was not always random. It also was highly organised, its chief aim to reduce the population to fewer than two million; to a single generation untainted by the old life. "If you want to live," the Khmer Rouge cadres told the townspeople. "you must surround your lives with silence. Hear nothing, know nothing, understand nothing."

The rules were explicit. People would live in collective farms, in straw-roofed barracks without walls, so that they could be watched all the time. They would be fed according to how "productive" they were, and this usually meant a tin of rice—the size of a small Nescafe tin—twice a week. An opaque—eyed woman, with her grief locked inside her, tells me that she was forced to go into the fields at night, leaving her six-month-old baby without a roof or food or care of any kind; in two days she returned to find the baby dead.

"Can you imagine they take away friendship?" says a young woman . . .

Only the camp "controller" could sanction marriage and husband and wife were permitted to meet only once a month. For the price of extra food and life, young boys were recruited as spies and listened from the rafters for laughter or sorrow. Anybody falling asleep during a midnight "ideological" lecture was denied a week's rations, or killed. Even the word itself—sleep—was banned; from Year Zero there would be only "rest".

Two men remain directly responsible for bombing Cambodia into the chaos that contributed to the rise of the Khmer Rouge; indeed, they bombed this land literally back to the Stone Age. One of them, Richard Nixon was disgraced in 1974 for domestic crookedness. The other, Henry Kissinger, received the Nobel Peace Prize and is still feted as a statesman.

The legacy of them all is a famine so severe that, in the words of one of the few relief officials here, "we have just six months to save three million people."

A generation ago, while the civilised world still reeled in disgust at Auschwitz, the United Nations was formed "so that this might never happen again."

IT HAS HAPPENED AGAIN.

Reading

Fill in the blanks with the appropriate words or phrases:

Cambodia lies to the west of ...... and, in ...... had a population of .... By ...... up to 3 million people had perished. One of the main reasons for this was the ...... of Cambodia by ...... in .... It resulted in the overthrow of ...... and allowed ...... to seize power. They wanted to create a society with no class and no modern ...... and this meant that the population had to be .... They declared 1975 .... They emptied the capital, ..., and forced the population to live in camps where even the expression of ...... was forbidden. The ...... was deliberately reduced and only with the invasion of Cambodia by ...... in ...... did the cold-blooded ...... finally stop.

Talking/Writing

1 What do you think Pilger's attitude is to the people who ordered the bombing of Cambodia? Try to find a few examples of the way he presents them and discuss why he presents them in this way.

2 How does Pilger convey his disgust with the Khmer Rouge through his choice of language? Find examples from his report.

3 From where did the Khmer Rouge get their ideas and what was their ideal society? Was there anything wrong with their ideals (as opposed to the way they carried them out)?

4 How does John Pilger bring home the scale of the murders? Choose several examples and explain why they make an impression on you.

5 Look at the layout of this piece — how do headlines, different sizes and types of print, photographs help to get Pilger's message across? Examine a few examples.

6 The Khmer Rouge were defeated from outside, not within their own country. Why do you think this was so? If only ten per cent of the population belonged to the Khmer Rouge, why didn't the others resist them? Was war justified in overthrowing the Khmer Rouge?
Try to discover why Vietnam invaded and what happened to Cambodia after the successful invasion.

7 Both Pilger and Kuper describe acts of genocide — wholesale slaughter of a people. Which of the pieces of writing has greater impact on you?
Why do you think this is so?

8 What would you say were the differences between the ideals of the Nazis and those of the Khmer Rouge?
Can you think of any other examples of genocide? Can you think of any which occurred *after* the defeat of the Khmer Rouge in 1979? What were the causes of the acts of genocide?

9 'IT HAS HAPPENED AGAIN.' Why does it happen again?

Hiroshima

by J. Steiner
(translated by Michael Hamburger)

At school the children hear a story,
they hear the story Hiroshima,
Hiroshima is a village in England.

Hiroshima was settled by Celts,
at Hiroshima things are not too good,
the farmers at Hiroshima are dissatisfied.

Hiroshima needs industry,
the children read out in chorus,
the teacher writes a word on the blackboard.

Talking

1 Mention the word 'Hiroshima' and, if it means anything to them at all, people think of the atom bomb, destruction, radiation, fire and death. Yet this poem is different. It seems to be full of false information. The language also seems rather childish.

Find examples of this false information and this childish language. Do you think it is supposed to be taken at face value or do you think it is meant to be treated *ironically*? What do you think the poet's attitude is to the events that *did* happen at Hiroshima and why doesn't he mention them in the poem?

2 What point do you think the poet is trying to make about the way we see the past and the way we learn about it? Who is to blame — the teacher, the children, neither, or both — and why? Try to justify your view, perhaps drawing on your own experiences. Perhaps you disagree with the poet — why?

3 Do you think war is inevitable? Why? Consider, if nuclear weapons are used in the next war, what are the chances that you — or perhaps your children — will learn about it in school afterwards?

Writing

Do a little research. Find out why the atom bomb was dropped on Hiroshima. Then write an essay explaining those reasons and discussing whether the reasons justified the deed.

Or

'Why War?'

Write an essay discussing the various causes of wars, making sure to refer to specific conflicts to illustrate the argument. How justified do you think war is as a means of solving our problems or achieving our ideals?

Or

'Can there be a just war?'
Are there any circumstances when *starting* a war can be right? What makes the cause 'right'?
Or
'A primitive act done with modern technology.'
Has the nature of war changed as our knowledge has advanced? Have the causes changed at all?

Extract from *When The Wind Blows* by Raymond Briggs

Hilda: If there really is going to be a War, who do you think will win?

Jim: Well, the Americans have Tactile Nuclear Superiority, due to their IBMs and their Polar Submarines, but in the event of a Pre-Emptive Strike, innumerate Russian hordes will sweep across the plains of Central Europe.... then the U.S. Technical Air Force will come roaring in with their Long Range Bombers—Superforts! B17s and B19s! Bristling with guns! Triffic they are! OK YOU GUYS! LET'S GO!...They'd razor the Russkie defences to the ground—then the Marines would parachute in and round up the populace.
After that, the big Generals would go over—like Ike and Monty, and then the Russians would capitalate and there would be a Condition of Surrender. Then they'd instil Free and Fair Elections, One Man-One Vote (and women too nowadays of course) and thus the Communist Fret to the Free World would be neutrified and democratic principles would be instilled throughout Russia—whether they liked it or not. .... That's the World Scenario as I see it, at this moment in time.

Talking/Writing

1 Which side do you think Jim supports? What makes you think this?
2 Is there anything in Jim's account that seems unlikely or unrealistic? Pick out and discuss any examples.
3 You may have noticed that Jim misuses some words. Pick out three examples. In each case explain what word Jim meant to use. What does this misuse tell us about Jim?
4 Many of the things Jim says are *clichés* — well used, well worn and predictable expressions. Pick out at least three examples and explain why you think they are clichés.
5 Why does Jim use so many capital letters when normally they would not be used?
6 What do all these things tell us about Jim and his grasp of the situation? Do you think the writer agrees with Jim? Defend your view!

Writing

Supply your own scenario (plan of situation and action) for any conflict which has occurred recently in the world.

1 Write your own World Scenario, outlining the broad divisions between various states and why these divisions exist.

2 Write the scenario for the start of a future conflict, establishing likely location, causes and outcomes.

Reading

Here is a further extract from *When The Wind Blows*.

Instead of looking to the future, it looks back to the past and shows how Jim and Hilda think of the Second World War. Perhaps the suffering and conflicts of the past can be a source of comfort and reassurance when they are all over. Consider *how* and *why* this could be. Can we use the past, our own past even, to keep our ideals alive or to revive them?

Talking/Writing

1 Look at the details Jim and Hilda choose to remember? Pick at least *four* examples and comment why they have remembered these particular details. Try to balance these details with ones that Jim and Hilda have missed out but which might also have been included in memories of the same war.

2 How, according to Jim and Hilda, does the present day differ from the past?

3 Look at the way the various leaders of the two sides are described and drawn. They are presented in a simplified and exaggerated form — known as *caricature.* Cartoonists often used this method of presenting characters to poke fun at them by making them seem ridiculous. It is found in written descriptions too.
What are the differences in the way the leaders of the two sides are described? Why are there differences between them?
Can you think why *caricature* might be useful in a war? Why it might be useful when outlining opinions, arguments or ideals?

4 Look at the list of memories at the end of the extract (perhaps your teacher will give you a burst of Vera Lynn Favourites to set the mood).
'Those were the days....' How does the choice of words contribute to the rosy picture of the war?

5 When we look back on our own past we often forget about the sadness or suffering we experienced. The reason for our first big row with our parents, the time we got lost by mum, the disasters of last year's holiday — these things don't seem quite so bad after a while.
Discuss a few occasions which seemed frightening or annoying or embarrassing at the time but now don't seem so terrible.

6 Sometimes when we look back, we see a world that was much simpler, when 'you knew where you stood'. But was it really like that? *Nostalgia* — a fond longing for the past — often leads to a simplification of what life was really like. Often people, like Jim and Hilda, idealise the past. Do you think nostalgia can influence the ideals that people have — and the way they see the present *ought* to be? Can war and suffering draw people together as well as dividing them? Can it reinforce ideals? Does it generate its own ideals?

Writing

Ask someone whom you know well and who is older than you about their childhood memories — perhaps of the Second World War itself. Write an account of their memories. Do you think they are idealised in any way?
Or
Design *two* posters, one for each side, which present the enemy faction as caricatures of evil and their own as examples of goodness. The two factions can be based on historical conflicts or they could be made up by yourself.

Unit
7

Future Imperfect

DYSTOPIA

A funny thing happened on our way to the twentieth century. . . . Well, you've studied the units, you know what it's all about. There, in some future Never-Never Land, was *Utopia*, the ideal, the perfect world. That was the target, Tomorrow's World. Get rid of prejudice, eliminate disease and poverty, stop killing one other in wars, waving our flags, beating our drums, and we'd find it just round the corner, next century, perhaps.

Then suddenly all the magic went out of it. Tomorrow's World went sour. Instead of reading about the wonders of Utopia we started shuddering at the grim prospects of *Dystopia*. Frightening futures of chromium-plated technology, drab worlds of nondescripts ruled by all-powerful anonymous figures,

BIG BROTHER IS WATCHING YOU.

And happiness, you remember happiness, that remote target? Well, happiness became a dirty word. You got your daily doze of the soma drug, a swig of Victory Gin — that kept you happy . . . and quiet . . . and docile . . . and unthinking. Happy . . . but somehow, less than human.

Talking

Why did this happen? Think of books, stories, films, you have encountered where a rather dismal or frightening world of the future is forewarned.

Has our experience of the achievements of technology something to do with it? The growth of a powerful Science Fiction? It's a very complicated issue, but you should first of all try to establish what experience you have of literature and film that takes a gloomy look at the future. (And I don't mean being dominated by aliens.) Secondly, see if you can make some suggestions as to why this should have happened.

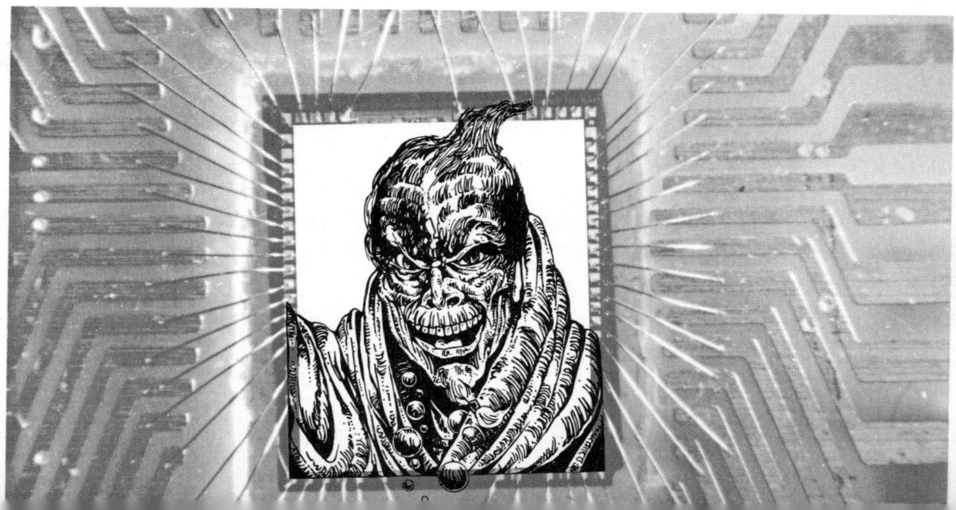

Eugenesis

by William McIlvanney

On the first day They eradicated war.
Nations were neutralized. In desert places
The cumbered void rusted with defused bombs
The gutted chambers. In random heaps
The rockets lay, like molar monuments
To brontosauri sentenced to extinction.

On the second day They fed the starving.
The capsules gave immunity from hunger.
Faces filled. The smiles were uniform.
The computers had found a formula for plenty.

The third day ended work. With summer
Processed to a permanence, the sun-
Machine in operation, every day
Would be as long as They desired it.
Season-chambers were erected. The nostalgic
Could take a holiday to autumn if they wished.
The computers thought of everything.

On the fourth day death was dead.
Synthetic hearts, machine-tooled brains,
Eyes and limbs were all expendable.
Immortality came wrapped in polythene.
Every face was God's you saw upon the street.

By the fifth day crime was cured.
Mind-mechanics, They located every hatred,
Extracted it, and amputated angers.
Each idea was sterilized before its issue.
The computers fixed a safety-mark for thinking.

The sixth day saw heaven's inauguration.
Benignity pills were issued. Kindness meetings
Were held on every corner. They declared
Love as the prerogative of all.
That day became the longest there had been.
But as long as there was light the people smiled.

On the seventh day, while They were resting
A small man with red hair had disappeared.
A museum missed a tent. Neither was found.
He left an immortal wife, the changeless years
Of endless happiness, and a strange note
In ancient script, just four historic letters.

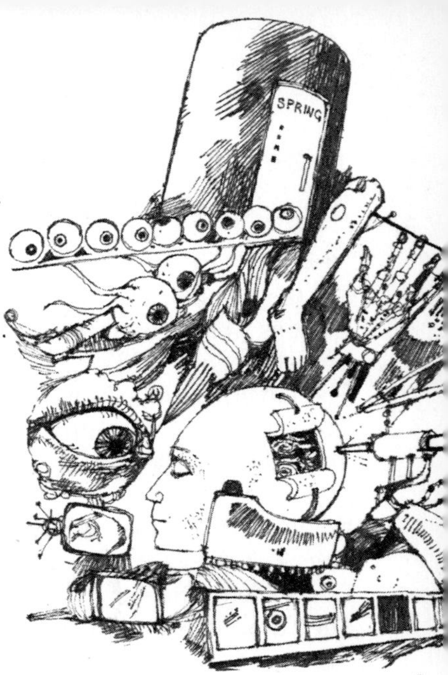

The Autotongue translated: 'Irrational Anger.'
The Medic Machine advised: 'Rejection Symptoms.
Source Unknown. Primordial and Contagious.'

It was too late. The word ran like a rash
On walls and daubed on doorways. Cities emptied.
In panic They neglected Their machines.
The sunset was unauthorized. Its beauty
Triggered the light-oriented metal cocks
That crew until their mechanisms burst.
Fires twinkled in the new night, shaping mattocks.
On the dark hills an unheavenly sound was heard.
The Historometer intoned into the silence:
'Ancient Barbaric Custom Known as Laughter.'
Seizing up, the computers began to cry.

The Horses

by Edwin Muir

Barely a twelvemonth after
The seven days' war that put the world to sleep,
Late in the evening the strange horses came.
By then we had made our covenant with silence,
But in the first few days it was so still
We listened to our breathing and were afraid.
On the second day
The radios failed; we turned the knobs; no answer.
On the third day a warship passed us, heading north,
Dead bodies piled on the deck. On the sixth day
A plane plunged over us into the sea. Thereafter
Nothing. The radios dumb;
And still they stand in corners of our kitchens,
And stand, perhaps, turned on, in a million rooms
All over the world. But now if they should speak,
If on a sudden they should speak again,
If on the stroke of noon a voice should speak,
We would not listen, we would not let it bring
That old bad world that swallowed its children quick
At one great gulp. We would not have it again.
Sometimes we think of the nations lying asleep,
Curled blindly in impenetrable sorrow,
And then the thought confounds us with its strangeness.
The tractors lie about our fields; at evening
They look like dank sea-monsters couched and waiting.
We leave them where they are and let them rust:

'They'll moulder away and be like other loam.'
We make our oxen drag our rusty ploughs,
Long laid aside. We have gone back
Far past our fathers' land.
And then, that evening
Late in the summer the strange horses came.
We heard a distant tapping on the road,
A deepening drumming; it stopped, went on again
And at the corner changed to hollow thunder.
We saw the heads
Like a wild wave charging and were afraid.
We had sold our horses in our fathers' time
To buy new tractors. Now they were strange to us
As fabulous steeds set on an ancient shield
Or illustrations in a book of knights.
We did not dare go near them. Yet they waited,
Stubborn and shy, as if they had been sent
By an old command to find our whereabouts
And that long-lost archaic companionship.
In the first moment we had never a thought
That they were creatures to be owned and used.
Among them were some half-a-dozen colts
Dropped in some wilderness of the broken world,
Yet new as if they had come from their own Eden.
Since then they have pulled our ploughs and borne our
loads
But that free servitude still can pierce our hearts.
Our life is changed; their coming our beginning.

Reading (Literature)

Compare McIlvanney's use of the 7-day timescale with Muir's employment of the same device.
What is the 'target' that each poet is aiming to hit?
State which poem you prefer, giving reasons for your choice.

The Unknown Citizen

by W. H. Auden

(To JS/07/M378 This Marble Monument is Erected by the State)

He was found by the Bureau of Statistics to be
One against whom there was no official complaint,
And all the reports on his conduct agree
That, in the modern sense of an old-fashioned word, he was a saint,
For in everything he did he served the Greater Community.

Except for the War till the day he retired
He worked in a factory and never got fired,
But satisfied his employers, Fudge Motors Inc.
Yet he wasn't a scab or odd in his views,
For his Union reports that he paid his dues,
(Our report on his Union shows it was sound)
And our Social Psychology workers found
That he was popular with his mates and liked a drink.
The Press are convinced that he bought a paper every day
And that his reactions to advertisements were normal in every way.
Policies taken out in his name prove that he was fully insured,
And his Health-card shows he was once in hospital but left it cured.
Both Producers Research and High-Grade Living declare
He was fully sensible to the advantages of the Instalment Plan
And had everything necessary to the Modern Man,
A phonograph, a radio, a car and a frigidaire.
Our researchers into Public Opinion are content
That he held the proper opinions for the time of year;
When there was peace, he was for peace; when there was war, he went.
He was married and added five children to the population,
Which our Eugenist says was the right number for a parent of his generation.
And our teachers report that he never interfered with their education.
Was he free? Was he happy? The question is absurd:
Had anything been wrong, we should certainly have heard.

Reading (Literature)

'Auden's *The Unknown Citizen* is satiric social comment.'
Discuss this in such a way as to show you fully understand the poem—and the meaning of 'satiric social comment'.

The Man in Asbestos: An Allegory of the Future

by Stephen Leacock

I could feel my senses leaving me. In the room across the hall there was a man singing. His voice, that had been loud, came fainter and fainter through the transom. I fell into a sleep, the deep immeasurable sleep in which the very existence of the outer world was hushed. Dimly I could feel the days go past, then the years, and then the long passage of the centuries.

Then, not as it were gradually, but quite suddenly, I woke up, sat up, and looked about me.

Where was I?

Well might I ask myself.

I found myself lying, or rather sitting up, on a broad couch. I was in a great room, dim, gloomy, and dilapidated in its general appearance, and apparently, from its glass cases and the stuffed figures that they contained, some kind of museum.

Beside me sat a man. His face was hairless, but neither old nor young. He wore clothes that looked like the grey ashes of paper that had burned and kept its shape. He was looking at me quietly, but with no particular surprise or interest.

'Quick,' I said, eager to begin; 'where am I? Who are you? What year is this; is it the year 3000, or what is it?'

He drew in his breath with a look of annoyance on his face.

'What a queer, excited way you have of speaking,' he said.

'Tell me,' I said again, 'is this the year 3000?'

'I think I know what you mean,' he said; 'but really I haven't the faintest idea. I should think it must be at least that, within a hundred years or so; but nobody has kept track of them for so long, it's hard to say.'

'Don't you keep track of them any more?' I gasped.

'We used to,' said the man. 'I myself can remember that a century or two ago there were still a number of people who used to try to keep track of the year, but it died out along with so many other faddish things of that kind. Why,' he continued, showing for the first time a sort of animation in his talk, 'what was the use of it? You see, after we eliminated death—'

'Eliminated death!' I cried, sitting upright. 'Good God!'

'What was that expression you used?' queried the man.

'Good God!' I repeated.

'Ah,' he said, 'never heard it before. But I was saying that after we had eliminated Death, and Food, and Change, we had practically got rid of Events, and—'

'Stop!' I said, my brain reeling. 'Tell me one thing at a time.'

'Humph!' he ejaculated. 'I see, you must have been asleep a long time. Go on then and ask questions. Only, if you don't mind, just as few as possible, and please don't get interested or excited.'

Oddly enough the first question that sprang to my lips was—

'What are those clothes made of?'

'Asbestos,' answered the man. 'They last hundreds of years. We have one suit each, and there are billions of them piled up, if anybody wants a new one.'

'Thank you,' I answered. 'Now tell me where I am?'

'You are in a museum. The figures in the cases are specimens like yourself. But here,' he said, 'if you want really to find out about what is evidently a new epoch to you, get off your platform and come out on Broadway and sit on a bench.'

I got down.

As we passed through the dim and dust-covered buildings I looked curiously at the figures in the cases.

'By Jove!' I said, looking at one figure in blue clothes with a belt and baton, 'that's a policeman!'

'Really,' said my new acquaintance, 'is *that* what a *policeman* was? I've often wondered. What used they to be used for?'

'Used for!' I repeated in perplexity. 'Why, they stood at the corner of the street.'

'Ah, yes, I see,' he said, 'so as to shoot at the people. You must excuse my ignorance,' he continued, 'as to some of your social customs in the past. When I took my education I was operated upon for social history, but the stuff they used was very inferior.'

I didn't in the least understand what the man meant, but had no time to question him, for at that moment we came out upon the street, and I stood riveted in astonishment.

Broadway! Was it possible? The change was absolutely appalling! In place of the roaring thoroughfare that I had known, this silent, moss-grown desolation. Great buildings fallen into ruin through the sheer stress of centuries of wind and weather, the sides of them coated over with a growth of fungus and moss! The place was soundless. Not a vehicle moved. There were no wires overhead — no sound of life or movement except, here and there, there passed slowly to and fro human figures dressed in the same asbestos clothes as my acquaintance, with the same hairless faces, and the same look of infinite age upon them.

Good heavens! And was this the era of the Conquest that I had hoped to see! I had always taken for granted, I do not know why, that humanity was destined to move forward. This picture of what seemed desolation on the ruins of our civilization rendered me almost speechless.

There were little benches placed here and there on the street. We sat down.

'Improved, isn't it,' said the man in asbestos, 'since the days when you remember it?'

He seemed to speak quite proudly.

I gasped out a question.

'Where are the street cars and the motors?'

'Oh, done away with long ago,' he said; 'how awful they must have been. The noise of them!' and his asbestos clothes rustled with a shudder.

'But how do you get about?'

'We don't,' he answered. 'Why should we? It's just the same being here as being anywhere else.' He looked at me with an infinity of dreariness in his face.

A thousand questions surged into my mind at once. I asked one of the simplest.

'But how do you get back and forwards to your work?'

'Work!' he said. 'There isn't any work. It's finished. The last of it was all done centuries ago.'

I looked at him a moment open mouthed. Then I turned and looked again at the grey desolation of the street with the asbestos figures moving here and there.

I tried to pull my senses together. I realized that if I was to unravel this new and undreamed-of future, I must go at it systematically and step by step.

'I see,' I said after a pause, 'that momentous things have happened since my time. I wish you would let me ask you about it all systematically, and would explain it to me bit by bit. First, what do you mean by saying that there is no work?'

'Why,' answered my strange acquaintance, 'it died out of itself. Machinery killed it. If I remember rightly, you had a certain amount of machinery even in your time. You had done very well with steam, made a good beginning with electricity, though I think radio energy had hardly as yet been put to use.'

I nodded assent.

'But you found it did you no good. The better your machines, the harder you worked. The more things you had the more you wanted. The pace of life grew swifter and swifter. You cried out, but it would not stop. You were all caught in the cogs of your own machine. None of you could see the end.'

'That is quite true,' I said. 'How do you know it all?'

'Oh,' answered the Man in Asbestos, 'that part of my education was very well operated—I see you do not know what I mean. Never mind, I can tell you that later. Well, then, there came, probably almost two hundred years after your time, the Era of the Great Conquest of Nature, the final victory of Man and Machinery.'

'They did conquer it?' I asked quickly, with a thrill of the old hope in my veins again.

'Conquered it,' he said, 'beat it out! Fought it to a stand-still! Things came one by one, then faster and faster. In a hundred years it was all done. In fact, just as soon as mankind turned its energy to decreasing its needs instead of increasing its desires, the whole thing was easy. Chemical Food came first. Heavens! The simplicity of it. And in your time thousands of millions of people tilled and grubbed at the soil from morning till night. I've seen specimens of them—farmers, they called them. There's one in the museum. After the invention of Chemical Food we piled up enough in the emporiums in a year to last for centuries. Agriculture went overboard. Eating and all that goes with it, domestic labour, housework—all ended. Nowadays one takes a concentrated pill every year or so, that's all. The whole digestive apparatus, as you knew it, was a clumsy thing that had been bloated up like a set of bagpipes through the evolution of its use!'

I could not forbear to interrupt. 'Have you and these people,' I said, 'no stomachs—no apparatus?'

'Of course we have,' he answered, 'but we use it to some purpose. Mine is largely filled with my education—but there! I am anticipating again. Better let me go on as I was. Chemical Food came first; that cut off almost one-third of the work, and then came Asbestos Clothes. That was wonderful! In one year humanity made enough suits to last for ever and ever. That, of course, could never have been if it hadn't been connected with the revolt of women and the fall of Fashion.'

'Have the Fashions gone,' I asked, 'that insane, extravagant idea of—' I was about to launch into one of my old-time harangues about the sheer vanity of decorative dress, when my eye rested on the moving figures in asbestos, and I stopped.

'All gone,' said the Man in Asbestos. 'Then next to that we killed, or practically killed, the changes of climate. I don't think that in your day you properly understood how much of your work was due to the shifts of what you called the weather. It meant the need of all kinds of special clothes and houses and shelters, a wilderness of work. How dreadful it must have been in your day—wind and storms, great wet masses — what did you call them? — clouds — flying through the air, the ocean full of salt, was it not? — tossed and torn by the wind, snow thrown all over everything, hail, rain — how awful!'

'Sometimes,' I said, 'it was very beautiful. But how did you alter it?'

'Killed the weather!' answered the Man in Asbestos. 'Simple as anything — turned its forces loose one against the other, altered the composition of the sea so that the top became all more or less gelatinous. I really can't explain it, as it is an operation that I never took at school, but it made the sky grey, as you see it, and the sea gum-coloured, the weather all the same. It cut out fuel and houses and an infinity of work with them!'

He paused a moment. I began to realize something of the course of evolution that had happened.

'So,' I said, 'the conquest of nature meant that presently there was no more work to do?'

'Exactly,' he said, 'nothing left.'

'Food enough for all?'

'Too much,' he answered.

'Houses and clothes?'

'All you like,' said the Man in Asbestos, waving his hand. 'There they are. Go out and take them. Of course, they're falling down — slowly, very slowly. But they'll last for centuries yet, nobody need bother.'

Then I realized, I think for the first time, just what work had meant in the old life, and how much of the texture of life itself had been bound up in the keen effort of it.

Presently my eyes looked upward: dangling at the top of a moss-grown building I saw what seemed to be the remains of telephone wires.

'What became of all that,' I said, 'the telegraph and the telephone and all the system of communication?'

'Ah,' said the Man in Asbestos, 'that was what a telephone meant, was it? I knew that it had been suppressed centuries ago. Just what was it for?'

'Why,' I said with enthusiasm, 'by means of the telephone we could talk to anybody, call up anybody, and talk at any distance.'

'And anybody could call you up at any time and talk?' said the Man in Asbestos, with something like horror. 'How awful! What a dreadful age yours was, to be sure. No, the telephone and all the rest of it, all the transportation and inter-communication was cut out and forbidden. There was no sense in it. You see,' he added, 'what you don't realize is that people after your day became gradually more and more reasonable. Take the railroad, what good was that? It brought into every town a lot of people from every other town. Who wanted them? Nobody. When work stopped and commerce ended, and food was needless, and the weather killed, it was foolish to move about. So it was all terminated. Anyway,' he said, with a quick look of apprehension and a change in his voice, 'it was dangerous!'

'So!' I said. 'Dangerous! You still have danger?'

'Why, yes,' he said, 'there's always the danger of getting broken.'

'What do you mean?' I asked.

'Why,' said the Man in Asbestos, 'I suppose it's what you would call being dead. Of course, in one sense there's been no death for centuries past; we cut that out. Disease and death were simply a matter of germs. We found them one by one. I think that even in your day you had found one or two of the easier, the bigger ones?'

I nodded.

'Yes, you had found diphtheria and typhoid, and, if I am right, there were some outstanding, like scarlet fever and smallpox, that you called ultra-microscopic, and which you were still hunting for, and others that you didn't even suspect. Well, we hunted them down one by one and destroyed them. Strange that it never occurred to any of you that Old Age was only a germ! It turned out to be quite a simple one, but it was so distributed in its action that you never even thought of it.'

'And you mean to say,' I ejaculated in amazement, looking at the Man in Asbestos, 'that nowadays you live for ever?'

'I wish,' he said, 'that you hadn't that peculiar, excitable way of talking; you speak as if everything *mattered* so tremendously. Yes,' he continued, 'we live for ever, unless, of course, we get broken. That happens sometimes. I mean that we may fall over a high place or bump on something, and snap ourselves. You see, we're just a little brittle still—some remnant, I suppose, of the Old Age germ—and we have to be careful. In fact,' he continued, 'I don't mind saying that accidents of this sort were the most distressing feature of our civilization till we took steps to cut out all accidents. We forbid all street cars, street traffic, aeroplanes, and so on. The risks of your time,' he said, with a shiver of his asbestos clothes,'must have been awful.'

'They were,' I answered, with a new kind of pride in my generation that I had never felt before, 'but we thought it part of the duty of brave people to—'

'Yes, yes,' said the Man in Asbestos impatiently, 'please don't get excited. I know what you mean. It was quite irrational.'

We sat silent for a long time. I looked about me at the crumbling buildings, the monotone, unchanging sky, and the dreary, empty street. Here, then, was the fruit of the Conquest, here was the elimination of work, the end of hunger and of cold, the cessation of the hard struggle, the downfall of change and death—nay, the very millennium of happiness. And yet, somehow, there seemed something wrong with it all. I pondered, then I put two or three rapid questions, hardly waiting to reflect upon the answers.

'Is there any war now?'

'Done with centuries ago. They took to settling international disputes with a slot machine. After that all foreign dealings were given up. Why have them? Everybody thinks foreigners awful.'

'Are there any newspapers now?'

'Newspapers! What on earth would we want them for? If we should need them at any time there are thousands of old ones piled up. But what is in them, anyway; only things that *happen*, wars and accidents and work and death. When these went newspapers went too. Listen,' continued the Man in Asbestos, 'you seem to have been something of a social reformer, and yet you don't understand the new life at all. You don't understand how completely all our burdens have disappeared. Look at it this way. How used your people to spend all the early part of their lives?'

'Why,' I said, 'our first fifteen years or so were spent in getting education.'

'Exactly,' he answered; 'now notice how we improved on all that. Education in our day is done by surgery. Strange that in your time nobody realized that education was simply a surgical operation. You hadn't the sense to see that what you really did was to slowly remodel, curve and convolute the inside of the brain by a long and painful mental operation. Everything learned was reproduced in a physical difference to the brain. You knew that, but you didn't see the full consequences. Then came the invention of surgical education — the simple system of opening the side of the skull and engrafting into it a piece of prepared brain. At first, of course, they had to use, I suppose, the brains of dead people, and that was ghastly' — here the Man in Asbestos shuddered like a leaf — 'but very soon they found how to make moulds that did just as well. After that it was a mere nothing; an operation of a few minutes would suffice to let in poetry or foreign languages or history or anything else that one cared to have. Here, for instance,' he added, pushing back the hair at the side of his head and showing a scar beneath it, 'is the mark where I had my spherical trigonometry let in. That was, I admit, rather painful, but other things, such as English poetry or history, can be inserted absolutely without the least suffering. When I think of your painful, barbarous methods of education through the ear, I shudder at it. Oddly enough, we have found lately that for a great many things there is no need to use the head. We lodge them — things like philosophy and metaphysics, and so on — in what used to be the digestive apparatus. They fill it admirably.'

He paused a moment. Then went on:

'Well, then, to continue, what used to occupy your time and effort after your education?'

'Why,' I said, 'one had, of course, to work, and then, to tell the truth, a great part of one's time and feeling was devoted towards the other sex, towards falling in love and finding some woman to share one's life.'

'Ah,' said the Man in Asbestos, with real interest. 'I've heard about your arrangements with the women, but never quite understood them. Tell me; you say you selected some woman?'

'Yes.'

'And she became what you called your wife?'

'Yes, of course.'

'And you worked for her?' asked the Man in Asbestos in astonishment.

'Yes.'

'And she did not work?'

'No,' I answered, 'of course not.'

'And half of what you had was hers?'

'Yes.'

'And she had the right to live in your house and use your things?'

'Of course,' I answered.

'How dreadful!' said the Man in Asbestos. 'I hadn't realized the horrors of your age till now.'

He sat shivering slightly, with the same timid look in his face as before.

Then it suddenly struck me that of the figures on the street, all had looked alike.

'Tell me,' I said, 'are there no women now? Are they gone too?'

'Oh, no,' answered the Man in Asbestos, 'they're here just the same. Some of those are women. Only, you see, everything has been changed now. It all came as part of their great revolt, their desire to be like the men. Had that begun in your time?'

'Only a little,' I answered; 'they were beginning to ask for votes and equality.'

'That's it,' said my acquaintance, 'I couldn't think of the word. Your women, I believe, were something awful, were they not? Covered with feathers and skins and dazzling colours made of dead things all over them? And they laughed, did they not, and had foolish teeth, and at any moment they could inveigle you into one of those contracts! Ugh!'

He shuddered.

'Asbestos,' I said (I knew no other name to call him), as I turned on him in wrath, 'Asbestos, do you think that those jelly-bag Equalities out on the street there, with their ash-barrel suits, can be compared for one moment with our unredeemed, unreformed, heaven-created, hobble-skirted women of the twentieth century?'

Then, suddenly, another thought flashed into my mind—

'The children,' I said, 'where are the children? Are there any?'

'Children,' he said, 'no! I have never heard of there being any such things for at least a century. Horrible little hobgoblins they must have been! Great big faces, and cried constantly! And *grew*, did they not? Like funguses! I believe they were longer each year than they had been the last, and—'

I rose.

'Asbestos!' I said, 'this, then, is your coming Civilization, your millennium. This dull, dead thing, with the work and the burden gone out of life, and with them all the joy and the sweetness of it. For the old struggle—mere stagnation, and in place of danger and death, the dull monotony of security and the horror of an unending decay! Give me back,' I cried, and I flung wide my arms to the dull air, 'the old life of danger and stress, with its hard toil and its bitter chances, and its heartbreaks. I see its value! I know its worth! Give me no rest,' I cried aloud—

'Yes, but give a rest to the rest of the corridor!' cried an angered voice that broke in upon my exultation.

Suddenly my sleep had gone.

I was back again in the room of my hotel, with the hum of the wicked, busy old world all about me, and loud in my ears the voice of the indignant man across the corridor calling, . . . 'Come down to earth.'

I came.

Reading

1 Write a paragraph in which you describe Asbestos and the people like him. You should base your description firmly on information given in the story, dividing your time between *what they look like* and *what they are*.

2 The writer makes Asbestos explain in some detail how the following were eliminated:

a) work,
b) climate/weather changes,
c) death,
d) the drudgery of learning/education.

In your own words, explain how any *three* of the above were eventually wiped out.

Choose *one* of the three and explain what Asbestos mentioned as a consequence of its elimination. What was *your* reaction to that consequence?

3 There are also a number of things Asbestos states have been eliminated where he doesn't go into such detail. In fact, you may suspect that the writer has introduced these items to poke fun at the *present* rather than being really worried about the *future*.

What tongue-in-cheek comment does the writer offer on each of the following:
a) fashion,
b) children,
c) newspapers,
d) war,
e) love and marriage?

4 There are also three areas where Asbestos clearly mentions that we even at this moment have gone some way towards his future solution.
a) in our use of machinery/technology,
b) in eliminating disease,
c) in the struggle for equality for women.
Taking these one at a time, explain why the particular item has been mentioned in this way.

5 What is the meaning of the word 'millenium'?

6 'I had taken it for granted, I do not know why, that humanity was destined to move forward.'
Here the narrator implies it hadn't! But if Asbestos' century had eliminated work, death, disease, etc. — in what sense has humanity *not* progressed?

Writing

Write a paragraph describing Broadway as you imagine it is *now*. (It doesn't matter if you are accurate.) You must describe it in order to bring out as clearly as you can the contrast with what it has become in Asbestos' world.

Talking

1 What Asbestos has lost — almost, but not quite — is *emotion*. Do you agree?
2 'Almost, but not quite . . .' Can you point to two examples where Asbestos shows a trace of feeling?
3 Is this story suggesting that, in fact, we need to *feel* things — pain, love, hunger, weariness, greed, fear — in order to be fully alive, fully human? Would you agree with that point of view?
4 In your opinion, are our *feelings* even more important to us than our *intelligence/reason*, as far as just being human is concerned?
5 Without feelings, even feeling unpleasant and terrifying emotions, are we just pretty smart robots?

Writing

Some lunatic who obviously doesn't know you has invited you to give 'The Epilogue' on television.

Greatly stirred by your reading of, and thinking about, this story, you decide to talk to your millions of viewers on what gives humans their humanity. You choose as your text, 'Give me no rest . . . .'

Write the short talk you would give.

Unit 8

PERFECTION CITY?

'Ghostly Understanding'

That's how John Wyclif defined *allegory* in the fourteenth century. Which tells us, at least, that allegory is a very old technique. And 'ghostly understanding' isn't a bad way of thinking about how it works. You are reading a story and suddenly realise that there's another story being told in the background. You become aware of another presence, or story, a bit insubstantial at first, and you are 'haunted' by a feeling of this other story going on in the background. You end up, as it were, reading two stories simultaneously. You realise that the events and characters in one story are symbols of events and people and ideas in that other 'ghostly' narrative. Usually, you find that this second story has some point, some message, to put across.
Read this little poem, for example. (How not to get on with one another.)

A Parable

by William Soutar

Two neighbours, who were rather dense,
Considered that their mutual fence
Was more symbolic of their peace
(Which they maintained should never cease)
If each about his house and garden
Set up a more substantial warden.
Quickly they cleared away the fence
To build a wall at great expense;
And soon their little plots of ground
Were barricaded all around:
Yet still they added stone to stone,
As if they never would be done,
For when one neighbour seemed to tire
The other shouted: Higher! Higher!
Thus day by day, in their unease,
They built the battlements of peace
Whose shadows, like a gathering blot,
Darkened on each neglected plot,
Until the ground, so overcast,
Became a rank and weedy waste.

Now in obsession they uprear;
Jealous, and proud, and full of fear;
And, lest they halt for lack of stone,
They pull their dwelling-houses down.
At last, by their insane excess,
Their ramparts guard a wilderness;
And hate, arousing out of shame,
Flares up into a wondrous flame:
They curse; they strike; they break the wall
Which buries them beneath its fall.

Talking

1 Who or what are the two neighbours? List, step by step, their behaviour with regard to the wall. What happens in the end?

2 Now, what does this little story make *you* think about? War? International politics? Nuclear deterrents?

3 What are the *emotions* that the poet thinks led to the 'insane excess'? (The important thing to note at this point is how you reacted to this very simple story. How soon did you sense it was *allegorical*? What the *allegory* was? Were you sort of 'double reading'?)

How to Read an Allegory

The best way to tackle this is to understand what goes on in our minds when we read an allegory. (Think back to the poetry parable you discussed.)

We start off reading a story, often a rather simple or unlikely sort of tale. 'Wait a minute!' our mind says. '*This* or *that* in this story reminds me of X or Y.' We sense, that is, *correspondences* and *analogies*.

correspondence:- relationship of agreement, part to part, one to one.

analogy:- agreement in certain respects between things otherwise different; resemblance of relations; parallelism; relation in general.

It is this correspondence that puts us on the track. For a time, having 'twigged' what's going on, we are reading the story in front of us and *translating* it into this other story or significance, simultaneously. By the time we reach the end of the story we started with, the 'ghostly' story or 'understanding' is dominating our attention. And that after all was the writer's aim.

1 We start off reading a story.
2 We become aware of the existence of correspondence.
3 We find ourselves reading two parallel stories.
4 We realise the significance of the second disguised story, the 'ghostly understanding'.
5 We can, on this basis, proceed to 'work out' the full *allegory*.

Allegory is the narrative description of a subject under the guise of something parallel.

Classic examples are John Bunyan's *Pilgrim's Progress*, George Orwell's *Animal Farm*, Richard Adams' *Watership Down*.

Extract from *Perfection City*
by David Shellan

SCENE: *The backcloth suggests a wide sweep of prairie with distant hills. On stage, to the right, a covered wagon whose frontier days are almost done. To the left, some scraps of vegetation suggesting a spring, near which sprawls* DEADBEAT, *his face covered entirely by an enormous hat. Beside him, the remains of a camp fire.* HOMBER *is pacing yards and calculating. Both are hobos and dress accordingly. Boxes, tins, pots and other rubbish are strewn across the stage. The lighting is brilliant white, suggesting heat. Towards the end of the play it mellows, suggesting dusk.*

HOMBER: [*without looking round*]: Say, Deadbeat. [*No response. More sharply*] Deadbeat.

DEADBEAT: [*moving hat sufficiently to uncover mouth*]: Yugh?

[*A monosyllable to strike despair to any heart less formidable than* HOMBER'*s*]

HOMBER: The city hall'll be right here.

DEADBEAT: Say, Homber, when do we eat?

HOMBER: Between the library and the concert hall.

DEADBEAT: Culture gives me indigestion.

HOMBER: This'll be the city centre. Gee, it makes me feel kinda warm inside.

DEADBEAT: [*scratching himself*]: Ya like horsemeat?

HOMBER: Sure I like horsemeat.

DEADBEAT: That was the last horse we had back at the border where I got these goddam itches. Ya like prairie dog?

HOMBER: Ain't particular.

DEADBEAT: [*lifting object vaguely resembling a rat*]: That's what we got. Cooked or cold?

HOMBER: Guess I ain't all that hungry.

DEADBEAT: Guess I ain't too.

[*Pause*]

Say, how far d'ya think it is to Frisco?

HOMBER: Frisco? That's a sinful town.

DEADBEAT: [*delighted*]: Yugh. Sure is sinful.

HOMBER: We ain't gonna go to Frisco.

DEADBEAT: Gotta go some place.

HOMBER: We're stopping right here.

DEADBEAT: I can't wait to get to Frisco.

HOMBER: I said we're stopping right here.

DEADBEAT: They got dames in Frisco.

HOMBER: Deadbeat, we're stopping right here.

DEADBEAT: They call 'em Frisco friskies. Shucks, they're some sheilas.

HOMBER: [*exasperated, shaking him*]: Here, ya wacky-eared moron, right here.

DEADBEAT: Don't shake me, ya lousy mixed-up Republican.

HOMBER: Well I'm trying to tell ya and all ya do is talk about sin.

DEADBEAT: Say, you got something better to talk about?

HOMBER: Sure have. Perfection, Deadbeat. This is it. We're stopping right here.

DEADBEAT: [*surveying auditorium*]: Perfection? Guess I'm kinda short-sighted.

HOMBER: In the middle of the great prairie right under God's own sun.

DEADBEAT: [*settling down again*]: Happy noo year.*

HOMBER: [*indicating the spring*]: There's water.

DEADBEAT: Way down.

HOMBER: And virgin earth.

DEADBEAT: Nothing could be virginer.

HOMBER: [*ecstatic*]: So this is where our city shall be. Perfection City, United States of America.

DEADBEAT: [*scratching*]: Stop it, Homber. You're making me uncomfortable.

[HOMBER *brings from the wagon a crudely made board reading, in indifferent lettering, 'Welcome to Perfection'*]

DEADBEAT: [*getting up, alarmed*]: Homber, ya're not serious?

HOMBER: Sure am.

DEADBEAT: What, here?

HOMBER: Right here.

DEADBEAT: In the middle of a goddam desert?

HOMBER: How many times have I told ya? Ya gotta have vision.

DEADBEAT: [*looking round again*]: Yugh. Sure have.

HOMBER: I'm telling ya, fifty years from now this city will be heaven on earth.

DEADBEAT: Yugh. And look what happened to Heaven-on-Earth, Nebraska. That was going fine for just a coupla days.

HOMBER: The ideal wasn't wrong, Deadbeat.

DEADBEAT: No, the land just didn't happen to be ours. Know what they're building there now? The State pen.

HOMBER: That's a place won't be needed in Perfection. We're gonna have a library instead.

DEADBEAT: Ya gonna lock up drunks in a library?

HOMBER: There ain't gonna be no drunks.

DEADBEAT: No drunks? What'll the marshal do?

HOMBER: We ain't gonna need no marshal.

DEADBEAT: No marshal? Shucks, every goddam hobo in the country'll be here tomorrow.

HOMBER: Ya see, Perfection is gonna be a city where there's nothing but love. Every single critter loves every other critter and there ain't no hard words spoken. So what's the use of a marshal?

DEADBEAT: How about keeping the Injuns off?

HOMBER: There ain't gonna be no Injun-fighting in Perfection.

DEADBEAT: You say so?

HOMBER: The constitootion says so.

DEADBEAT: Aw shucks, we got one of them?

HOMBER: It's the very first thing we gotta have.

DEADBEAT: The Injuns gonna read it?

HOMBER: Sure they're gonna read it. The Injuns'll belong to Perfection. Perfection belongs to every critter. God loves every goddam hobo.

DEADBEAT: Injun city, ugh?

HOMBER: Injun and hobo, hobo and Injun. Brudders under the prairie sky. Ain't that wonderful?

DEADBEAT: [*ironic*]: Yugh, that's wonderful.*

HOMBER: Every critter'll have equal rights.

DEADBEAT: Have what?

HOMBER: Equal rights.

DEADBEAT: Where d'ya pick that up?

HOMBER: Ya never heard of Jefferson?

DEADBEAT: [*looking ruefully at his bare feet*]: Was he the skunk pinched ma boots back in Indiana?

HOMBER: No critter pinched ya boots. They fell off. I keep telling ya. Jefferson was the greatest critter ever lived.

DEADBEAT: Then he ought to have got boots of his own.

HOMBER: He'd got boots of his own. Will ya shut up about boots? I don't wanna hear about boots. Your boots fell off in Indiana and that's the end.

[*Pause*]

DEADBEAT: Say, Homber.

HOMBER: [*who is bringing out junk from the wagon*]: Yugh?

DEADBEAT: This equal rights.

HOMBER: Yugh?

DEADBEAT: Does it include boots?

HOMBER: Sure it includes boots.

DEADBEAT: You got boots.

HOMBER: Sure I got boots. I live good.

DEADBEAT: I'm the only critter ain't got boots. Jefferson's gotta down on me.

HOMBER: Jefferson wasn't worried about boots. He worried about other things.

DEADBEAT: What did he worry about?

HOMBER: The constitootion.

DEADBEAT: [*dejected*]: I wanna go Frisco.

HOMBER: Listen. This critter Jefferson wrote the Declaration of Independence.

DEADBEAT: [*impressed*]: He could write?

HOMBER: Sure he could write. He was president.

DEADBEAT: Could he read as well?

HOMBER: Sure he could read.

DEADBEAT: I feel kinda stoopid. I can't go on.

HOMBER: It's just because of Jefferson ya can go on, ya lousy son of a bitch. All critters are created equal. That's what he said.

DEADBEAT: Did he say that?

HOMBER: Sure did. Wrote it down. All critters are created equal.

DEADBEAT: But you've got boots and I ain't.

HOMBER: [*exasperated*]: I got boots because I tie them on. That's why I got boots. Now come and help me build Perfection.

DEADBEAT: We gonna build it now?

HOMBER: Sure. No sense wasting time. [*Handing him a pile of wood*] Here, catch hold of this.

DEADBEAT: What is it?

HOMBER: It's the city hall.

DEADBEAT: [*after an uncomprehending pause*]: The what?

HOMBER: The city hall. The roof. [*Handing him another pile*] This is the floor. You can start.

DEADBEAT: I can start. I can start?

HOMBER: Building. Ya can start building.

DEADBEAT: [*gazing into the distance*]: Where can I start building?

HOMBER: [*pointing to his feet*]: Right there, clophead.

DEADBEAT: The city hall. Right here.

HOMBER: Right there.

[*Pause while* DEADBEAT *drops wood at his feet and examines it*]

DEADBEAT: Say, what goes in the city hall?

HOMBER: The big shots. Critters who run the place.

DEADBEAT: We gonna have big shots?

HOMBER: Gotta have someone to organise.

DEADBEAT: Who they gonna be?

HOMBER: Well, guess we gotta have a president to start with.

DEADBEAT: What's he do?

HOMBER: He signs the constitootion.

DEADBEAT: I can't write.

HOMBER: Then I declare myself elected.

DEADBEAT: You?

HOMBER: By a landslide.

DEADBEAT: Since when could you write?

HOMBER: We gotta have schools. This ignorance is goddam appalling. We gotta teach these hobos. I wanna sign the constitootion right now.

[DEADBEAT *begins to look for the constitution*]

Deadbeat, the constitootion ain't written yet.

DEADBEAT: That so? Well, you go right ahead and write it.

HOMBER: I can't. It ain't constitootional. The president signs it. Some other critter's gotta write it.

DEADBEAT: There ain't no other critter.

HOMBER: There's you, ya moron.

DEADBEAT: Now listen to me, I'm no moron. Besides, I can't write.

HOMBER: You gotta start learning. You're the noo saccertaria state.

DEADBEAT: The noo what?

HOMBER: Saccertaria state.

DEADBEAT: Who says so?

HOMBER: I say so.

DEADBEAT: I ain't been elected.

HOMBER: Ya don't have to be elected. I appoint you.

DEADBEAT: Ya do?

HOMBER: Because I'm president. [*As* DEADBEAT *sits again*] What are ya squatting for now?

DEADBEAT: [*scratching*]: I'm thinking.

HOMBER: We ain't got time—

DEADBEAT: I don't give a bellyache about the time. Things are happening to me. I gotta think, else I'll grow up ignorant. And my big toe hurts.

[*An arrow appears in the 'Welcome' board*]

HOMBER: What was that?

DEADBEAT: Yugh, must have been.

HOMBER: Sounded like—

DEADBEAT: Yugh, that's what I figured.

HOMBER: Goes to show how deceptive sounds can be.

DEADBEAT: Sure does.

HOMBER: Ya just can't trust no sound no place.

DEADBEAT: I'd never trust no sound nowise myself.

[*They see, and react to, the arrow simultaneously*]

Say, Homber.

HOMBER: Yugh?

DEADBEAT: D'ya suppose this has any significance?

HOMBER: Yugh. Guess it does.

DEADBEAT: What d'ya suppose it signifies?

HOMBER: Injuns.

DEADBEAT: I kinda thought that's what you'd say.

HOMBER: It's the Injun's way of commoonicating.

DEADBEAT: [*backing slowly*]: Injun and hobo, hobo and Injun, just wrapped up together, ya said?

HOMBER: Sure. Just perfect love.

DEADBEAT: Homber.

HOMBER: Yugh?

DEADBEAT: Frisco's this way.

HOMBER: We ain't gonna go to Frisco.

DEADBEAT: I just feel kinda lonesome.

HOMBER: We're not quitting now, yallerback.

DEADBEAT: I just feel kinda attached to my scalp.

[DEADBEAT *has now reached the wings where* CAWAWEEKAW, *a tall brave with bare torso, is standing motionless behind him. As* DEADBEAT *slowly backs into him, he is gagged and his hands tied with wholly theatrical rapidity*]

HOMBER: [*unaware*]: The Injuns are my constitooents, Deadbeat. If they wanna commoonicate they can go right ahead.

CAWAWEEKAW: Brother, I speak peace.

HOMBER: Ugh?

CAWAWEEKAW: I speak peace.

HOMBER: [*delighted*]: He speaks American. Our first vote.

CAWAWEEKAW: Learn lingo from former scalps.

HOMBER: [*checked*]: Of course, we don't know which way.

CAWAWEEKAW: Speak American extremely well. Goddam critter and lousy son of a bitch.

HOMBER: Say, you've been listening.

CAWAWEEKAW: Name, Cawaweekaw.

HOMBER: Come again?

CAWAWEEKAW: Cawaweekaw.

HOMBER: That's quite an achievement. Would you mind very much letting go the lousy lump of horsemeat ya got there?

CAWAWEEKAW: [*indicating Deadbeat*]: This?

HOMBER: Yugh, that. I guess it's not much but it's kinda all I got.

[DEADBEAT, *released, runs towards* HOMBER *but is jerked back by the rope held by* CAWAWEEKAW. HOMBER *pulls gag from mouth*]

DEADBEAT: [*howling*]: Homber, scratch me urgently.

HOMBER: [*doing so*]: I keep telling ya, ya should look where ya sit.

DEADBEAT: It don't matter where I sit. They kinda travel with me.

HOMBER: Listen. We'll give this naked critter an interview. You're the interpreter.

DEADBEAT: The what?

HOMBER: All ya gotta do is tell me what the critter says.

DEADBEAT: But he speaks the lingo—he said so.

HOMBER: It ain't dignified for a president to speak direct. Tell him he's welcome to Perfection, the city of brotherly love.

DEADBEAT: [*to Cawaweekaw*]: You're sure welcome to it.*

CAWAWEEKAW: Land here—tribe's.

HOMBER: Well, go on, Deadbeat—interpret.

DEADBEAT: [*adding elaborate gestures*]: Land here, tribe's.

HOMBER: Tell him the president ain't fixed the city boundary yet.

DEADBEAT: No city boundary.

CAWAWEEKAW: No city.

DEADBEAT: Says there's no city. Pretty fast thinker.

HOMBER: Tell him the city'll be here in a day or two.

DEADBEAT: City here pretty soon.

CAWAWEEKAW: Beg to differ, et cetera.

HOMBER: [*delighted*]: Ya see? He's had a business education.

CAWAWEEKAW: [*suddenly communicative*]: Dear sir, extremely interested in bizniz. Listen, will tell. White man once come to red man's camp. Fur-lined boots. Beeeg bizniz.

HOMBER: What became of him?

CAWAWEEKAW: Use scalp as typewriter cover.

HOMBER: Business men never stay one place long. Like me and Deadbeat, till today. Now we're gonna go no place. We're stopping right here.

CAWAWEEKAW: You say?

HOMBER: Sure I say. We're gonna build Perfection. It's all in the wagon.

CAWAWEEKAW: You have wagon full of perfection?

DEADBEAT: It's fulla rotten wood.

HOMBER: Deadbeat, where's ya vision?

DEADBEAT: That's where I got these goddam itches, from that lousy hunk.

HOMBER: Ya gotta have vision to build Perfection. Ya gotta see it clean and clear like a blue sky. Gotta see it as it will be. A place we can live in like buddies, way out here on the prairie. Ya gotta admit, it's a great ideal.

CAWAWEEKAW: [*sharpening hatchet on what looks like a strop fixed to a belt*]: Most great.

HOMBER: You think Jefferson be proud of me?

CAWAWEEKAW: You say?

HOMBER: Jefferson, Greatest critter ever lived.

CAWAWEEKAW: Regret not officially informed.

HOMBER: We sure need schools in Perfection. Say, I gottan idea.

DEADBEAT: Aw, shucks, no.

HOMBER: Say we start Perfection with a big celebration? Get all the folk in the city centre with a big bonfire and a big dance? Say, can you dance, Deadbeat?

DEADBEAT: [*indignant*]: Ma boots were pinched in Indiana.

HOMBER: What's the matter with the bare feet God gave ya?

DEADBEAT: The big toe hurts.

CAWAWEEKAW: Me dance extremely well.

HOMBER: That so?

CAWAWEEKAW: See. [*He does a few steps*]

HOMBER: Guess that's good. How about that, Deadbeat?

DEADBEAT: It ain't commercial.

HOMBER: It'll do fine. We gotta have originality. D'ya know any other Injuns with party pieces?

CAWAWEEKAW: Tribe have interesting and absorbing hobby. Collect war dances.

HOMBER: Say, that's wonderful. We'll call them peace dances. We'll have the city centre here—just an open space with flowers and fountains and cute little statues, like in Liquor Town, Ohio. And the Injuns can come on to the square and do their peace dance.

CAWAWEEKAW: See, will demonstrate. [*He capers round the 'Welcome' board*]

HOMBER: Say, can we join in?

CAWAWEEKAW: Follow me.

HOMBER: Whoopee.

[*As they scamper round,* CAWAWEEKAW *seizes the rope and pulls in* DEADBEAT, *whose hands no-one has remembered to untie. He quickly involves* HOMBER *in the tangle and ties both of them to the board.* HOMBER *faces away from* CAWAWEEKAW]

Say, that dance is sure something. That dance'd sure be a hit back in Boston. Is this how it ends?

CAWAWEEKAW: Always.

HOMBER: Kinda captivating, Deadbeat, ugh?

DEADBEAT: I'd rather not think too much just now, Homber, d'ya mind.

HOMBER: What happens now?

CAWAWEEKAW: Braves dance round.

HOMBER: Say, we'll have a ringside seat.

CAWAWEEKAW: [*again sharpening hatchet*]: Other braves make preparations.

DEADBEAT: Homber.

HOMBER: Yugh?

DEADBEAT: Guess it's too late to go to Frisco.

HOMBER: That's it, we're stopping right here.

DEADBEAT: That's the way I feel.

HOMBER: Perfection's gonna be just lovely, Deadbeat, I can see it now.

DEADBEAT: What I can see ain't so lovely.

HOMBER: You gotta have vision, I keep telling ya.

DEADBEAT: I got vision all right.

HOMBER: We've been looking for Perfection for a mighty long time, me and you, Deadbeat. Been right across this land of promise but it's been worth getting here.

DEADBEAT: Then you'll die happy, Homber.

HOMBER: Shucks, I ain't begun living yet. Perfection's made me a noo man. Say, what's the Injun doing now? Is it all over?

DEADBEAT: Yugh, very soon.

HOMBER: Is he gonna cut us loose?

DEADBEAT: Yugh, that's right. Gonna cut us loose.

[*But* CAWAWEEKAW's *advance is interrupted by sudden gunshots*]

CAWAWEEKAW: [*drawing back*]: White men.

HOMBER: Do I hear shooting?

CAWAWEEKAW: Regret must withdraw.

HOMBER: Shooting's not permitted in Perfection.

CAWAWEEKAW: Regret unable prolong visitation.

HOMBER: Say, you're not going?

[*More shots*]

CAWAWEEKAW: Reluctantly compelled.

HOMBER: Drop in any time.

CAWAWEEKAW: You too kind. Thanking you for esteemed favours, yours faithfully.

[*More shots. Exit* CAWAWEEKAW *hurriedly*]

HOMBER: Say, Deadbeat, when ya start writing that constitootion put in something about noise, will ya?

[*More shots*]

There's gonna be no noise in Perfection.

DEADBEAT: No noise.

HOMBER: Nothing but beautiful clean silence.

[*Enter* JOHN JEFFERSON JACKSON, *almost entirely covered by ammunition belts. Two revolvers in hand, another in belt*]

JACKSON: [*shouting*]: Come back, ya lousy yaller son of a bitch, I wanna fill ya full of lead.

HOMBER: And no swearing. Make that the next goddam law.

JACKSON: Just you show ya cringing copper-hoofed yaller face, ya deadalive Injun. [*Fires into the air*] Just you wait till ya feel the noo machine gun. It'll chop ya legs off inside of a minute.

HOMBER: Critters will love each other. That's law number three.

JACKSON: What's this then? Two-legged movables laced up? Perfection? Gee, these salesmen don't waste much time.

HOMBER: Glad to know ya. My name's Homber.

JACKSON: Hi. Who's ya friend?

HOMBER: That's Deadbeat.

JACKSON: That ain't a name, it's a description. I'm John Jefferson Jackson.

DEADBEAT: Homber — he must be the skunk pinched my boots.

JACKSON: Little man, did I hear you say skunk?

DEADBEAT: B-b-back in Indiana.

JACKSON: I ain't been to Indiana for years. Not since the railroad came out west. That's my job, the railroad. Been chasing Injuns all day. What did you say your name was?

HOMBER: I'm Homber. I'm the president.

JACKSON: Yugh? What of?

HOMBER: This city.

JACKSON: What city?

HOMBER: The city we're gonna build here. Perfection.

JACKSON: You gonna build it?

HOMBER: Me and Deadbeat.

JACKSON: Yugh?

HOMBER: Wanna help?

JACKSON: I tell ya, I'm on the railroad.

HOMBER: Me and Deadbeat, then.

JACKSON: [*having cut them loose by now*]: Listen, fella. I ain't got time to play games. There ain't gonna be no city here.

HOMBER: Who says so?

JACKSON: Railroad boss, that's who says so. Railroad boss says where the cities go. If ya don't wanna job with the railroad, ya gotta clear off out. Okay?

HOMBER: I ain't moving. I'm building Perfection right here.

DEADBEAT: Say, steady, Homber. The guy's offering us a job.

JACKSON: You used to work?

DEADBEAT: We've had our disagreements.*

JACKSON: On this job ya live rough and work hard.

DEADBEAT: Any dough?

JACKSON: A kinda rumour.

DEADBEAT: Any chance getting to Frisco?

JACKSON: If ya don't get mislaid by Injuns.

DEADBEAT: That figures.

JACKSON: Like the one nearly had ya then. We're gonna build a fort here, so the railroad comes right through.

HOMBER: A fort? Here in Perfection?

JACKSON: To fight the Injuns.

HOMBER: You're gonna fight them?

JACKSON: Only way to stop them fighting us. Listen, son, I like ya. I'm giving ya the chance to go dream some place else. Mighty soon we're gonna rip through those belly-aching yallerbacks like a knife in the guts. We gotta noo kinda machine gun — wait till ya hear —

HOMBER: [*turning away in pain*]: I don't wanna hear.

JACKSON: [*bewildered*]: But I tell ya, it's scientific.

HOMBER: I don't wanna hear. We're building our city right where you're standing and there ain't gonna be no guns at all.

JACKSON: Be sensible, will ya —

HOMBER: We're gonna build Perfection in this place and in no other.

JACKSON: Brudder, that sure is rash talking. [JACKSON *crosses to* DEADBEAT *and rolls a wad of notes in front of him*] Say, fella, remember how to eat?

DEADBEAT: The memory ain't so good.

JACKSON: You and ya baxy buddy gotta go and quick.

DEADBEAT: Gotta go?

JACKSON: [*handling gun*]: That's what I said.

DEADBEAT: I ain't disputing.

JACKSON: Take a few of these. It's called dough.

DEADBEAT: Yugh, I remember.

JACKSON: Enough for a square feed. D'ya want boots as well?

DEADBEAT: It'd be kinda convenient.

JACKSON: Get a job with the railroad.

DEADBEAT: Where?

JACKSON: [*pointing right*]: Way back.

DEADBEAT: [*pointing left*]: What's that way?

JACKSON: The mountains. Injuns. No food. No place to handle dough. Plenty of space for two corpses. If ya're not outa here in five minutes, you'll be getting in the way.

DEADBEAT: So ya said.

JACKSON: I'll be back. If you're not as baxy as your friend I'll see ya later on the railroad — that way. [*He makes to go off right, but hesitates and turns to* HOMBER *as if impelled to explain*] Listen, fella. Mebbe what we do ain't right but who's the hobo knows right from wrong? If we don't kill the Injuns, they kill us. Your skin or mine—and brudder, there's no choice in that. [*A parting shot to* DEADBEAT] Five minutes, critter.

[*Exit* JACKSON. *There is a pause while* DEADBEAT *packs their garbage into the wagon. Lights dim slightly to suggest a sinking sun*]

DEADBEAT: [*gently*]: Homber. Gotta move, ya lousy old coyote. Gotta saddle* up and jog on over. [*Pause*] You still sore? It was a mighty good idea while it lasted. So what? It lays itself down and dies, just like every other goddam thing on this stinking earth. [*Pause*] Guess there'll be jobs for both of us on the railroad, Homber. That's food and sleep kinda regular. Guess I might get boots. That's kinda something. Might even be noo ones.

HOMBER: [*who has been motionless, gazing leftwards*]: Say, Deadbeat.

DEADBEAT: Yugh?

HOMBER: What d'ya see way over there?

DEADBEAT: Just mountains.

HOMBER: What's it like in the mountains?

DEADBEAT: Cold, I guess.

HOMBER: Yugh. Cold and kinda clean.

DEADBEAT: Well, guess we're all set. Coming, Homber?

HOMBER: Say, Deadbeat, in those mountains there'd be water. And good soil, mebbe, virgin earth. Right up there in the mountains there'd be a place for Perfection, Deadbeat, some little valley, right away from everything, some little place to build our city. [*He takes over the wagon and pulls it to the left*]

DEADBEAT: But, Homber, listen—

HOMBER: Whatya waiting for, clophead? We gotta go build Perfection in the mountains.

DEADBEAT: [*looking right*]: But the railroad—food and sleep—

HOMBER: Ya gotta choose, Deadbeat.

DEADBEAT: Homber, listen, gimme time to think.

HOMBER: I ain't got time to wait. Perfection's not the waiting sort of city. Are ya coming?

DEADBEAT: [*torn between the two sides of the stage*]: It's just that I'd kinda like* to have boots.

HOMBER: [*starting off*]: So long, Deadbeat.

DEADBEAT: [*a cry*]: Homber, don't leave me.*

HOMBER: [*stopping*]: You gonna come?

DEADBEAT: Guess I gotta have something more than just boots.*

HOMBER: [*delighted*]: You gonna help me build Perfection?

DEADBEAT: [*with him now at the wagon*]: I guess we can build Perfection any goddam place — if anyone'll let us.

[*They move off*]

Talking

Well, obviously, the play is set in America. Is it *about* America? Remember Homber's words — 'So this is where our city *shall be.* Perfection City, United States of America.' And later, 'been right across *this land of promise.*' Is Perfection City what America *should* be ideally? If so, what stands for it as it is?

Homber is obviously an idealist, and perhaps rather an 'impractical person'. (See definitions, Unit 1.) So what does that make Deadbeat? And Cawaweekah, what does he symbolise? And John Jefferson Jackson? The railroads, yes. But what do the railroads stand for? Big business? Vested interests? Capitalism? Is there a link between this and how Cawaweekah speaks?

Writing/Talking

Working in pairs, see if you can copy out and complete this very simple grid, to see if the class can establish some general agreement.

Perfection City	
San Francisco	
Homber	
Deadbeat	
Cawaweekah	
Jackson	

At this stage, keep answers brief and simple. All we want is to establish what basic correspondences you see.

Now, as soon as you begin to recognise your basic correspondences, two things happen:

1) you start to see what it all means,

2) you begin to see smaller correspondences that knit into the general allegory.

Talking

1 Is it all about the reality of American life compared to the ideals set out in the American Constitution?

2 Is it asking about Perfection City being attainable on earth at all? (Think what happened to Heaven-on-Earth, Nebraska.)

3 Is it about the stupidity of idealism?

4 How do the Indians fit into this? And the bosses of the railroad?

5 And the smaller correspondences? Deadbeat's boots? What about the meaning of the mountains at the end?

Reading

See if you can copy out the following table, making your answers as full as you can, trying to fix your ideas as clearly as possible.

In the first column are characters, incidents, quotations, details. In the second column, comments on the *meanings* you feel correspond to these. In one or two cases, both columns have been completed for you as examples to follow.

Reference	**Meaning**
1 Homber	The idealist, though not very well-organised. 'You gotta have vision to build Perfection, Ya gotta see it clean and clear like a blue sky. Gotta see it as it will be. A place we can live in like buddies ......'
2 Deadbeat (on the other hand)	
3 Cawaweekah	
4 John Jefferson Jackson	Gun-happy, prejudiced. Represents railroad, big-business, who in real life dictate what life is all about, where and how people live it. 'Railroad boss says where the cities go.'
5 Heaven-on-Earth, Nebraska	
6 'Brudders under the prairie sky'... 'hobo and injun, injun and hobo...'	Represents...
7 'Jefferson wasn't worried about boots. He worried about other things.'	Perhaps this suggests that..
8 Deadbeat: 'But you've got boots and I ain't.' Homber: 'I got boots because I tie them on.'	This short interchange tells us that...
9 'Then I declare myself elected.'	This suggests...

10	Cawaweekah, in saying this, asserts *his* right to the land, rejecting Homber's offer of Perfection City.
11	These things represent to Deadbeat (a) the pleasures of life, (b) the necessities of life.
12 Cawaweekah: 'Tribe have interesting and absorbing hobby. Collect war dances.' Homber: Say that's wonderful. We'll call them peace dances.'	
13 'We're gonna build a fort here...'	
14 'Say, Deadbeat, in those mountains there'd be water. And good soil, mebbe, virgin earth. Right up there.... in the mountains there'd be a place for Perfection.'	

Reading (Literature)

In this play Deadbeat's answers give an important series of clues to his character and attitudes. Study them carefully, then state clearly what each tells you about Deadbeat. Take the stage direction into account when one is given. (*Asterisked in text*)

1 (settling down again) 'Happy Noo Year.'

2 (ironic) 'Yugh, that's wonderful.'

3 (to Cawaweekah) 'You're sure welcome to it.'

4 'It ain't commercial.'

5 (to Jackson) 'We've had our disagreements.'

6 (gently) 'Homber, gotta move, ya lousy old coyote.. It was a mighty good idea while it lasted. So what? It lays itself down and dies, just like every other goddam thing in this stinking earth..'

7 (torn between the two sides of the stage) 'It's just that I'd kinda like to have boots.'

8 (a cry) 'Homber, don't leave me.'

9 'Guess I gotta have something more than just boots.'

Write an essay in which you discuss the following quotation, referring closely to the play to support your argument.

'The relationship between Homber and Deadbeat is an interesting one, only fully explained by the end of the play.'

"In *'Perfection City'* there is comedy — situation comedy, comedy of character, amusing dialogue. But, in the end, what it has to say is serious and important."

Do you agree? Try to cover all the points raised in the quotation, and refer to the play to support the points you raise.

This final project in this unit is really an exercise in reading the 'small print' of allegory.

I imagine that, like me, some of you felt that the actual name — John Jefferson Jackson — was rather odd. Why was it odd? Perhaps because the two names that this name was made out of were sort of familiar. If you thought that, you'd be quite right. Both Jefferson and Jackson were Presidents of the United States.

So what did I know about these two presidents of the United States? To be honest — not a thing! But I still had this hunch that the dramatist putting these two names together was more than just coincidence. So I looked them up.

Extract from *America. The Story of a Free People*

Jefferson delighted in people, and in seeing them contented whether efficient or not. His inefficiency as Governor of Virginia has been exaggerated, but . . . he was not a particularly efficient Secretary of State. But as a political thinker . . he was without a peer. When he suggested the inscription on his gravestone, he proposed . . . . his three major contributions to thought. The stone reads:

> HERE WAS BURIED THOMAS JEFFERSON
> AUTHOR OF THE DECLARATION OF AMERICAN INDEPENDENCE
> OF THE STATUTE OF VIRGINIA FOR RELIGIOUS FREEDOM
> AND FATHER OF THE UNIVERSITY OF VIRGINIA

Jefferson's great aim was to give individual men a wider liberty.

Jackson's main creed can be summed up in a few phrases:
Faith in the common man; belief in political equality; belief in equal economic opportunity; hatred of monopoly, special privilege, and the intricacies of capitalistic finance.

Did all of this help me? Did it enable me to understand more fully what the writer was getting at? Yes it did. But more importantly, has it helped *you*?

Reading (Literature)

Try to *a*) write a paragraph on John Jefferson Jackson as he seems now to fit into the allegory of the play, and *b*) write a paragraph explaining how expressions used to sum up the achievements of Jefferson and Jackson relate to the allegorical interpretation of the play as you see it. (E.g. 'not particularly efficient', 'University of Virginia', 'Declaration of American Independence', 'political equality', 'intricacies of capitalistic finance', etc. might seem relevant to you.)